MURDER
— IN —
STARK COUNTY
OHIO

KIMBERLY A. KENNEY

THE
History
PRESS

Published by The History Press
Charleston, SC
www.historypress.com

Courthouse image courtesy of the McKinley Presidential Library & Museum.

First published 2020

Manufactured in the United States

ISBN 9781467143028

Library of Congress Control Number: 2019954282

Notice: The information in this book is true and complete to the best of our knowledge. It is offered without guarantee on the part of the author or The History Press. The author and The History Press disclaim all liability in connection with the use of this book.

CONTENTS

ACKNOWLEDGEMENTS

I first met Amelia Richardson while researching grocery stores for my book *Stark County Food: From Early Farming to Modern Meals* with coauthor Barb Abbott. Amelia's husband, Edward, owned a grocery store in Massillon in the 1870s, which is why her story came up in my research. She was accused of killing him on January 17, 1876, which she said was self-defense. Edward was a prominent citizen in Massillon, so his murder caused quite a stir in the small community. I sort of fell down a rabbit hole that day in September 2017, desperate to read all I could about her. I wasn't sure how or when, but I knew that I was going to tell her story. I am excited that I found a way to share it with you.

Amelia was the catalyst for this book, which recounts murders in Stark County from 1833 to 1906. I have left it to others to write about more modern murders and murderers. My fascination is mostly confined to the nineteenth century, when life was supposedly simpler and safer—yet people were killed anyway.

Most of the murders I've chosen to write about were committed by husbands, wives or girlfriends, but some were just acquaintances. In one case, a son poisoned his father. I have used contemporary accounts of each of the murders to write these stories. During most of the periods in which I am writing, there was more than one newspaper in Canton. In some cases, multiple perspectives from different newspapers provided an interesting look into who did and did not cover certain aspects of the story or how the story was covered. Lengthy transcripts from these trials were published in the pages of these newspapers, which is completely different from how a trial is covered today. As a historian, I am grateful for these journalists of the past, who are almost always unnamed.

One note on formatting: the *Repository*, Canton's paper of record since 1815, has been known by slightly different names over the years. To simplify the text, I have chosen to refer to it as the *Repository*, regardless of the era covered. I am indebted to Gary Brown for his meticulous research on the series of name changes over time.

1815–1826	*The Ohio Repository*
1826–1830	*The Ohio Repository and Stark County Gazette*
1830–1868	*Ohio Repository* or *The Ohio Repository*
1868–1874	*Canton Repository and Republican*
1874–1878	*The Canton Repository*
1878–1886	*The Canton Daily Repository* and *The Sunday Repository*
1886–1930	*The Evening Repository*, *The Sunday Repository*
1930	*The Evening Repository* and *The Canton Daily News*
1930–1939	*The Canton Repository* and *The Canton Daily News*
1939–1978	*The Canton Repository*
1978–2016	*The Repository*
2016–present	*The Canton Repository*, *The Sunday Repository*

Thank you to Gatehouse Media for permission to reprint several images from the *Repository* here. And thank you to Mandy Altimus Pond, archivist at the Massillon Museum, for her help in locating images of the Bammerlin family (Amelia's parents and brother).

I want to thank my legal consultant, attorney Cheryl Kraus, who helped me understand some of the more technical aspects of the drama in the courtroom. I also want to thank my science consultant, James Vergis, a scientist with a doctorate in molecular biophysics and biochemistry, who explained complicated scientific principles of blood analysis and poison to this historian. James and I have been friends for almost forty years, which does not seem possible.

This is the eighth book I've published, and I always use this space to thank my amazing family for their support in all of my endeavors: my grandmother Marjorie Vanderhoof; my mother, Cheryl Beach; and my sister, Kristen Merrill. I know I've said it before, but you truly are the best team of cheerleaders anyone could ask for! This time around, my mother and sister received chapters as I wrote them, and they were each anxiously awaiting the next installment. These stories have been so much fun to tell, and I know my readers will be drawn into each of them from the very first page, just like they were.

FINALLY, I WOULD LIKE to dedicate this book to the memory of my dear husband, Christopher Kenney, who passed away on Christmas Eve 2019 after a courageous battle with cancer. He left this world much too soon and will be missed by so many. This writer is left searching for words to adequately convey what he meant to me. Without him, I am adrift. But I know he is here with me, every minute of every day, forever.

INTRODUCTION

Why do the grisly details of a murder capture our imaginations? Why do the names of victims seem to fade with time, yet their killers often become household names? Why is true crime, in all its forms—TV shows, movies, books, magazines and podcasts—growing in popularity?

Writers and psychologists have spent considerable time ruminating on these questions. The answer is relatively simple: It's normal.

Writing for the companion blog of *Psychology Today* magazine on May 24, 2018, Robert T. Muller, PhD, said, "Forensic psychologist Paul G. Mattiuzzi contends that a fascination with murder is nothing out of the ordinary, and in fact, is practically built-in to people. Said plainly: 'The crime of murder is a most fundamental taboo and, also, perhaps, a most fundamental human impulse.' Mattiuzzi maintains that the allure comes from the many questions we ask ourselves—Why did they do it? Could I do that? Was there nothing that could have stopped this?" We are forced to look at ourselves through the lens of these crimes, and we hope when we do, we like what we see.

As a species, humans are fascinated by the idea of good versus evil, an idea at the very heart of true crime. "We want to figure out what drove these people to this extreme act, and what makes them tick, because we'd never actually commit murder," noted Erin McCarthy in her article "12 Reasons We Love True Crime, According to the Experts," published by *Mental Floss* on October 10, 2018. The struggle to understand "evil" and what it means be "good" are common themes in fiction. When the crimes we write about are true, it adds a dose of reality to a really good story. These things actually happened, in the places where we live. Real people died, and real people killed them. McCarthy suggests that true crime allows us to feel empathy—for both the victims and their killers. We want to understand why someone committed a crime, and how someone became their victim, even if it's only to prevent it from happening to us. Psychologists say we are drawn to true crime because we are thankful that we are neither the victim nor the perpetrator. There might even be an element of *schadenfreude*, getting enjoyment from trouble experienced by others, says Dr. Sharon Packer, a psychiatrist and assistant clinical professor of psychiatry and behavioral sciences at the Icahn School of Medicine at Mount Sinai. It isn't sadistic, necessarily—just a sense of relief that if it had to happen to someone, at least it wasn't you.

It might come down to simple biology. In the January 8, 2016 edition of *Time* magazine, Scott Bonn, criminology professor at Drew University and author of *Why We Love Serial Killers*, wrote:

> *People…receive a jolt of adrenaline as a reward for witnessing terrible deeds. Adrenaline is a hormone that produces a powerful, stimulating and even addictive effect on the human brain. If you doubt the addictive power of adrenaline, think of the thrill-seeking child who will ride a roller coaster over and over until he or she becomes physically ill. The euphoric effect of true crime on human emotions is similar to that of roller coasters or natural disasters. The public is drawn to true crime because it triggers the most basic and powerful emotion in all of us—fear. As a source of popular culture entertainment, it allows us to experience fear and horror in a controlled environment where the threat is exciting but not real.*

Regardless of why we are drawn to true crime, it has become big business. What started as a dime store paperback industry has grown to include wildly popular television shows like NBC's *Dateline* and podcasts like *Serial*.

This book explores murders that happened, quite literally, in our own backyard. Christian Bachtle became Stark County's first murderer in 1833, and over the years there have been many sensational crimes committed here. You may be familiar with the 1880 triple hanging of three teenage murderers or the dramatic trial of Annie George, who was accused of killing President McKinley's brother-in-law George Saxton in 1898. But there are some lesser-known murder cases that are just as fascinating, such as those of Amelia Richardson, Joseph Kline, George McMillan, Henry Popp and James Cornelius—none of which is a household name.

Many of the murderers, and their victims, are buried throughout Stark County. Although we speak the names of the killers more often, it is my hope that this book will help to preserve the memories of those who were killed.

May they all rest in peace.

1
CHRISTIAN BACHTLE

approached to her bed cautiously, probably, without her being aware of it. I struck her with the flat side of the axe-helve, a heavy blow on the side of the head and ear. I then took the infant from her breast, and laid it in bed with the other children." In his confession, written on November 14, 1833, and published a week after his execution by hanging in the *Repository* on November 29, Christian Bachtle told the world exactly how he killed his wife in the early morning hours of April 2 of that year. He continued, "As I took the babe from her, I heard her give a low moan or sigh, as though she were expiring, and I presume she was senseless. But thinking it possible she was still sensible to suffering, I thought it would be an act of mercy to despatch [*sic*] her at once. Accordingly, I struck her again with the sharp corner of the axe-helve." With that final blow, Mary Henry Bachtle became Stark County's first murder victim, and her husband became its first murderer.

Mary and Christian were married on April 13, 1826. He was twenty-three, and she was just fourteen. It was the first marriage for both of them, although Bachtle had lived out of wedlock with a woman named Betsey Morrison in Maryland, with whom he had a child who died the same day it was born. It was not a happy union. "The woman…like myself, was addicted to intoxication, and we had many unpleasant scenes together," he wrote. After two years, he left her and moved to Pennsylvania, where he became a day laborer for a time, before moving to Congress Furnace (present-day North Industry) in Stark County.

Soon after he arrived, Bachtle met Mary. For the next seven years, he worked for local farmers and distillers, mentioning Jacob Welty and Christopher Smith by name in his confession. During most of this time, according to Bachtle, the couple was happy, until the winter of 1833, when he began drinking heavily again. "I resorted too frequently to my cups—drank daily—and, when I was at home, with nothing on my hands, frequently got drunk," he said. He described Mary as "kind and affectionate," adding, "Had I done as well as she did, we might still have lived happily together—all might still have been well."

His drinking was common knowledge in the small community. Under the headline "Horrid Murder" in the April 5, 1833 edition of the *Repository*, Bachtle was described as "habitually intemperate." The article also claimed he "kept Whiskey in his house; that he drank on an average of more than quart a day; and when drunk was of a violent and vindictive temper." During his episodes of intoxication, Mary pleaded with her husband to reform, but in his confession, he maintained that she "never complained that I abused or misused her....Although she mourned over my errors, she never upbraided me. She did all that could be expected of a wife, in assisting to provide for and support our growing family." At the time of the murder, the couple had three children: Wilhelm (six), Mary Anne (four) and Caroline (two). Christian Bachtle said that he "loved her [his wife], ardently and devotedly, loved her, at least so far as one in my situation was capable of loving—and that my affection for her was the only reason why I was not sooner completely abandoned to gross intoxication."

In the months leading up to the murder, Bachtle's dependence on alcohol steadily increased. He was in debt to creditors who had begun harassing him for payment, and he frequently had thoughts of suicide. Through the cloud of his drunkenness, he thought Mary's "affections were alienated from me," though he added with the clarity of sobriety in jail, "Strange would it have been had they not become alienated," due to his increasingly erratic behavior.

About a month before the murder, he decided to hang himself. He walked into the fields with a rope but then abruptly changed his mind. "I had gone some distance when the thought suddenly suggested itself, unbidden, that my wife was the cause of my misery," he wrote in his confession, "and that she, not I, ought to die. The suggestion came with such force, that I immediately turned, as if with mechanical impulse, for the purpose of returning home, and at once ridding me of her, the cause of all my sufferings. But before I reached home, I became more tranquil, and took no steps towards carrying my design into execution."

But the thought, once formed, did not leave his mind. He became obsessed with the idea of killing her, which was intertwined with the notion that she no longer loved him. During the trial, several witnesses testified that Bachtle had told them he caught his wife having an affair with a man named Ezra Johns. In an article summarizing the trial testimony in the *Repository* on October 4, 1833, George Dunbar Esq. said, "I asked him the cause of his killing her; he said he had caught Ezra Johns with her 2 or 3 times; had in the day time looked through the window, and saw them on the bed together; caught them together afterwards in the stable." Under cross-examination, Dunbar added, "I told him I doubted his story about Johns and his wife, that habitual drunkards were apt to get jealous of their wives." In his confession, Bachtle admitted that he had "unjustly accused" Johns to try to justify his crime. Although he did not think she was unfaithful as he plotted to kill her, he was convinced that her "affections were altogether alienated from me."

On the day of the murder, Bachtle spent the afternoon working for his mother-in-law. He admitted he had been drinking but was not drunk. Mary was there too, and he said in his confession, "I thought the whole family, and my wife also, looked sour and disaffected towards me. But little was said by them, and as for me, I meditated murder—I resolved, during that afternoon, that in the evening, I would, if possible, test her feelings; and if they were not such as I could wish, I would take her life." On the way home from her mother's house that evening, and again when they arrived home, Mary and Bachtle argued, although the subject of the disagreement is not known. Later accounts claimed that he came home that evening and found her asleep in their bed, but his confession paints a different picture of the events that night.

As he had planned, he began to "test" Mary's devotion. He asked her when she was going to make him a pair of pantaloons, from the cloth he had purchased earlier that day, and she responded that she "would not make them at all." Bachtle persisted, saying that she took in laundry and sewing for other people, why not for her husband? She replied that other people paid her for her labor, but she "got no reward for anything she did" for him. He knew she was absolutely right about that, even in the moment, but still it made him angry. "I took a new made axe-helve," he said in his confession, "and laid it on the chimney before where she was sitting. If she saw me do it, which I think she did, she paid no attention to it, and, I presume, had no suspicion of any evil design on my part."

The couple went to bed between seven and eight o'clock that evening. They continued to argue, Bachtle recalling that she "went so far to declare that she would never have any more intercourse with me." He decided, in his heightened state of mind, that her refusal was evidence of her infidelity. He got up, walked to the fire and returned to bed. He spoke to her but did not elaborate on what he said in his confession. "Her answer was irritating," he said. He told her he was going to get dressed and leave. She didn't respond. What happened next would change all of their lives forever.

"I went to the chimney and took down the axe-helve," he said. "I walked back and forwards, from the bed to the fire, two or three times. She was lying with her back towards me, and her face to the wall. The infant was at her breast!" He struck her head with the axe handle so hard, the coroner concluded that her skull had been fractured and her ear was nearly cut off. "It was not until after I had struck the last blow, that I reflected on what I was doing, or had done," he said. "In a moment, however, after the fatal deed was done, remorse was let loose upon me. In the anguish of my heart, I cried out, 'Good God, what have I done!' and from the depth of my soul, I exclaimed 'God have mercy on you.' Worlds of wealth, had they been at my command, at that moment, would freely have been sacrificed, could they have restored her to life, and me to innocence."

And then he panicked. He looked in her pocket and found four dollars, which he took. He packed up a few of his personal belongings, a loaf of bread and a quart of "that curse of my existence—WHISKEY." He sat on a rock in a neighbor's yard, coming to terms with what had just happened. On one hand, he thought he should return to the scene of the crime and pay for what he had done. On the other hand, he convinced himself that he had done the right thing and should run. Steeling his resolve with a swig of whiskey, he took off across the fields.

As he was fleeing, he said he thought of his youngest child and, for a moment, considered going home to make sure she was all right. Again, he talked himself out of it. Around 2:00 a.m., he lay down and slept for about an hour. When he woke up, he ate some of his bread and realized he was lost. He started walking and eventually arrived at his brother-in-law John Moore's house. "When I first saw him," he said, "I hoped he would not know me, but he did, and I was obliged to stop with him a few minutes. On leaving him, I bent my course towards Wooster." The second night, he stayed in a private house. While he slept, there was a thunderstorm, and he dreamed that he was struck by lightning three times. He continued

Canton was a bustling town on the frontier at the time of Mary Bachtle's murder. This artist's rendering shows the intersection of Tuscarawas Street and Market Avenue, the geographic center of town. *Courtesy of the McKinley Presidential Library & Museum.*

heading toward the direction of Wooster, although he did not have any specific escape plan in mind.

In the meantime, Canton authorities were closing in on him. Warner Richards and a Mr. Nichols caught up to him, and he was arrested. The *Repository* was still a weekly in those days, so the first newspaper account of the crime was printed with an addendum to the original story, saying he had confessed. His trial began on September 30, and in his confession, Bachtle stated that the trial was "an impartial one, and the verdict of the Jury correct." He praised his attorneys, saying they did the best they could to defend him in the face of public opinion, which wanted to see him convicted and executed for his crime.

The *Repository* covered Bachtle's murder trial in great detail on October 4, 1833. The prosecuting attorney was D.A. Starkweather, with Dwight Jarvis assisting. Bachtle's defense lawyers were John Harris and O. Metcalf. Judges Lane and Wood heard the case, and the following men served as jurors: John Hoover, Peter Troxal, Peter M. Wise, Daniel Smith, Anthony Housel, John Houghton, Peter Deshong, Isaac Kootzner, Joseph Hewitt, Richard Vanderhoof, Valentine Weaver and John Raffensperger.

Mary's sister Margaret Henry was the first witness called. She testified that she arrived at the Bachtle residence at nine o'clock on Tuesday morning (April 2) and found her sister dead in her bed. At first, she did not see the wound. She said that Bachtle had been at her house the day before and said that it was the last day he would work with them, but she did not hear him say anything about planning to kill his wife. Under cross-examination, she said she was frequently at the Bachtle home and often heard them quarrelling. Her sister had not complained during the seven years she had been married to Bachtle until about two months before the murder, when she began saying that he was "scolding" her and drinking too much. It had gotten so bad she said she could not live with him if he continued on this path.

Next, Mary's brother, Jacob Henry, took the stand. He testified that his sister and Bachtle had come to his mother's house the day before the murder and had left together. He also heard Bachtle say he would not work for the family anymore and mentioned that Bachtle was thinking of "going over the mountains."

Then the prosecution called Thomas Worley, who testified that one of his hands alerted him to Mary's death that morning. When he got to the Bachtle residence, Mary's mother told him she was gone. "I felt the body, it was not warm, neither was it altogether cold; there was much blood in the bed." He could not say how long she had been dead. Worley testified both to the prosecutor and under cross-examination that he had never heard them quarrel but noted that he was not often at their home.

Mary's mother, Barbara Henry, was the next to testify. She corroborated what her daughter Margaret had said, that Bachtle had been a kind and affectionate husband until very recently and Mary had started to complain about his drinking and treatment of her. Barbara noted that she had known her son-in-law's mother for five years. "All that time she has been insane," she told the court. She said he was always kind to his children, but she had heard of his being jealous of his wife. "He accused her of infidelity in my presence," she said, but Mary denied it.

Then John Moore, Bachtle's brother-in-law, was questioned. He testified that Bachtle came to his house on the morning after the murder, when the sun was "an hour or two high." He said Bachtle told him his wife and children were well when he left the house, and he had stayed overnight at Anthony Housel's house. He seemed to be in a hurry and did not want breakfast. He said he was going to his brother Joseph's house. Under cross-examination, Moore said Bachtle had never been to his house before. He also corroborated Barbara Henry's testimony that Bachtle's mother was "deranged" in all of the ten to twelve years he had known her.

Warner Richards then testified that he saw Bachtle on April 3 eight or nine miles north of Wooster, on the road to Waynesburg in Wayne County. "I was in pursuit of him," he said. "He confessed to us immediately, that he had killed his wife, and said he was glad of it. He said he knew he would be hung for it, for it was deliberately done." Bachtle told Richards that he had been planning to kill her for five or six weeks. He also noted that Bachtle had a bottle of whiskey with him. Under cross-examination, Richards told the court that Bachtle said he was not sorry for what he had done. "He had asked for a favor in bed, the night of the murder, and she refused him," Richards said. Bachtle asked her twice, and she refused. He offered her thirty-seven and a half cents, and again she refused. He said he was trying to decide if he should just leave her to be with other men or kill her. According to Richards, Bachtle then struck her with his fist twice, killing her. Other witnesses also testified that he had used his fists. In his written confession, published in the *Repository*, Bachtle corrected this portion of the testimony. He said he had killed her swiftly, using the axe helve, not his fists, which would not have been as efficient. "The reason of my making this statement is that it has increased the distress of her friends, to think that she was sent out of this world, by a lingering death of torture and suffering," he said. "I can assure them that such is not the case. I am confident she was beyond the sufferings of this world, from the moment I inflicted the first blow."

The next witness called was John Saxton, founder of the *Repository*, who was part of the inquest held over the body. The wound was "about 2½ inches in length," he said, "from 2 to 2½ inches in depth. My impression is that it was on the left side of the head, and that the cap was drawn on that side. The front part of the wound was a square cut. [The] back part bone [was] broken so that pieces were taken out with a probe. The cap she had on was of calico and it was cut through. The hair was also cut. The wound could not have been caused with the fist. [It] must have been done with an axe or hatchet." Saxton also said an axe was found "with a handle in it newly scraped," but there was no blood on it. When he was cross-examined, Saxton added that there was no blood found throughout the house, only in the bed where Mary was found. After Dr. Alfred Heacock and Dr. Robert Estep both testified that the wound described could not have been inflicted with a fist, the prosecution rested.

Bachtle's primary defense was that he was generally a calm person, he was not able to control himself when he was drinking and he was possibly insane, which might be hereditary. Several witnesses spoke of bizarre behavior they had witnessed, and while some thought it was the result of his drinking, others did not. Bradley C. Goodwill was his first character witness. He testified that he had known Bachtle for about three years, and he had been "a very quiet and peaceable man, so far as I have heard or known." He estimated that Bachtle drank "probably a gallon a week," although he had never seen him so drunk that he was unable to work. His testimony continued:

> [I had] *at different times seen in* [the] *defendant peculiarities of conduct, that induced a belief of mental aberration, particularly on the morning of the 1ˢᵗ April. He came to settle with me. I told him he had lost considerable time while working with me, and did not know that I had better employ him any more. He said he had but a half day's job to do with any one, that was for his mother-in-law, then he would work for me constantly. He spoke of some kinds of work that he did not like to do. I told him if he did not like to work as I wanted, he had better stay away. He then said I had done a good deal for him, and he would not object to any thing. We made a contract for a year. He saw some pigs playing together.* [He] *said if they (alluding to his wife's sister and her husband) did as well as the pigs, they would do well enough. He was reaping for me once. In the after part of the day he acted strangely. I requested him to leave the field for fear of some accident. I did not think him drunk, or that his actions were the result of drinking.* [I] *thought it the effect of heat and hard labor. At another time he attended the court of Appeals. When he came home he was more deranged than I ever knew him before, or since.* [I] *thought liquor the cause. Tho' he acted differently from any other drunk man I ever saw.* [I] *have seen at other times, when I thought his aberration not the effect of liquor.*

Under cross-examination, Goodwill added, "I considered him insane on the 1ˢᵗ of April from peculiar language and manners. They were quite unusual. I saw him once as a witness before [George] Dunbar, when I thought he could not distinguish right from wrong."

Next, Bachtle's sister Lena Bachtle testified that three or four weeks before the murder, she had a conversation with Mary. Lena asked Mary if she was afraid of her husband. "She said she was not. He had always used her well, and she had no reason to be afraid. He had never struck her or lifted his hand against her. He had threatened other people who came to the house. She said he had always been kind and affectionate to the family." She added that their mother "has been deranged more than 30 years. [She] was so when the defendant was born."

Then a series of witnesses testified about his alcohol use and mental state. John Loop said he always kept liquor with him and could not work without it. Adam Smith recalled thinking Bachtle was deranged but never saw him drink. Daniel Flora saw him only once but thought he was intoxicated, rather than deranged. James S. Black told the following story in support of Bachtle's possible insanity:

> *Three of us went over to the house of his mother-in-law, in the evening, heard him in the woods talking to himself. We went down to his house and passed near where he was. I think he heard us. He kept quiet as we passed him. When we got to his house, his wife was crying about him. She requested us to bring him home.... We went back to his mother-in-law. He came there and talked foolish. [He] wanted to fight us. He got into a scuffle with [someone]. We separated them, and he soon became very good natured. [He] said it had done him good. We went home with him, and he treated us when we got there with whiskey. He had quite a quantity in a bottle. He had been working in the water for Goodwill, and I thought him intoxicated. I saw him again soon afterwards, at a distiller. He said he had been persuaded to quit drinking. [He] had not drank spirits for some time. He said it made him feel bad. A Mr. Brook came into the distillery and dunned* him for some money that he owed him. He became irritated and said he could not pay him. He said others were dunning him also. He could not pay. He took out his knife and requested Brook to cut off his head. He did not drink at the distillery. [He] said he had not drank for several days. I presumed he had not. The night I saw him in the woods, he talked about sheep. [He] thought himself chasing sheep. He also prayed and preached and sung.*

John Brown testified that he was working at Goodwill's still house once when Bachtle showed up. "When he came in he drew his fist, looked very mad, and threatened to strike me. Then he laughed, took off his hat and gave me two apples."

Dr. Robert Estep was again called to the stand to explain what could have caused Bachtle's apparent breaks with reality. "Mono Mania is distinguished from madness," he said, "generally, in this: that the subject is insane only on one or more subjects; not on all. A Mono Maniac may have correct perceptions and deranged judgements, or the reverse. It is generally temporary, and comes on by fits. Mania is frequently hereditary, and would usually, if so, appear in the subject at about the same age as it

---

* Dun means "to make persistent demands on someone, especially for payment of a debt."

did the ancestor. In Mono Mania the subject frequently reasons correctly from false perceptions. It frequently intermits. Drinking liquor might excite the disease. It frequently comes on suddenly, by a recurrence of a particular object, and the subject may be suddenly restored to sanity, by anything which causes a strong impression. It is often difficult to be detected." Dr. Alfred Heacock was the final witness, and he supported most of Dr. Estep's testimony. Bachtle did not take the stand in his own defense.

The state then recalled Barbara Henry, Margaret Henry, John Moore, John Dunbar and George Dunbar, who all testified that they had not seen Bachtle act in any way that could be considered insane. Additional witnesses corroborated this testimony: Betsey Kleckner, Christopher Smith, Catharine Moore and James H. Lee.

The jury deliberated for four hours before finding Bachtle guilty of murder in the first degree. The same edition of the *Repository* printed the sentencing, as pronounced by Judge Lane:

> *The crime of which you are convicted, is one of the deepest grade of those contained in our system of Jurisprudence, and is followed by the severest punishment.*
>
> *Listen to the sentence of the law—*
>
> *You shall be taken hence to the common [jail], and from thence, on Friday the 22d day of November next, between the hours of 10 in the morning, and 3 in the afternoon, you are to be taken to the place of execution, and there you shall be hanged by the neck until you are dead—and may God Almighty have mercy on your soul.*

In the days between his sentencing and his execution, Bachtle prepared his written confession, quoted earlier. In his conclusion, Bachtle waxed poetic about his fate: "I am a hateful outcast from society, treading on the borders of the Grave, and must soon, forever, close my eyes on all earthly scenes. The Sun and Moon shall continue to rise and set; winter and summer, seed time and harvest, come and return—all nature shall pursue its usual course, bring to other life, and light and activity, while I shall be sleeping in the grave."

He also used his confession as a cautionary tale about the perils of alcohol: "Avoid the intoxicating cup, as you would the enemy of your souls. To that I can safely trace my present condition. And, yet, this reflection brings no consolation, no ease, to my burthened spirit. It is not a wall of defence [*sic*] behind which the guilty soul can fly, for safety and support, in the hour of need."

The execution was covered in the same edition of the *Repository* in which his confession appeared. The writer noted that the media was not present, so they were relying on the "information of others who were present… being little inclined to look upon a scene so mortifying and degrading to human nature." The night before the execution, Canton was inundated with visitors from "miles around," many of whom could not find lodging for the evening and slept on the streets. Alarmed at the crowds, the town council ordered a watch patrol to keep the masses under control. "By break of day, the open space around the prison was so thronged as to render it necessary to guard the doors." Extra security guards from neighboring communities were called in to help:

> *At half past 10 the Light Companies commanded by Capts. Dunbar and Kelly, drew up before the prison, and 15 minutes after were joined by the Ravenna Troop of Cavalry, commanded by Col. Drake; the New Philadelphia Troop, commanded by Capt. Taylor, and the Canton Troop, commanded by Lieut. Beals. By this time, such was the denseness of the crowd around the jail, that the military were compelled to remove them at the point of the bayonet, after all other means had failed to effect that object.*

The crowd was estimated between thirty and forty thousand.

Bachtle was taken from the jail, "habited in his shroud," at eleven o'clock in the morning. He was accompanied by Reverend Monosmith of the German Presbyterian church, Reverend Swayze of the Methodist church, other clergymen, a few relatives, Dr. Haddock and Dr. Stidger. Bachtle requested, under the protection of the sherriff's deputies, to be allowed to walk to the place of execution, described as "the open squares east of Mrs. Nighman's Brewery," which was near the corner of North (present-day Sixth Street NE) and Rex Streets. It took thirty minutes to press through the dense crowd. While Bachtle sat on a chair placed on the gallows, the reverends led a prayer service, in both English and German, which concluded at two o'clock in the afternoon. Recalling the crime on the occasion of another execution for murder, the July 21, 1883 *Stark County Democrat* reported that Bachtle had "made a few remarks to the crowd, warning them of the evil influence of intoxicating drink and expressing an entire willingness to die." He sang a hymn, which he had personally selected, embraced the sheriff and ascended the gallows at 2:15 p.m. The *Stark County Democrat* described Bachtle's last moments:

After bidding an affectionate farewell to his attendants who then left the platform, Sherriff Webb pinioned his hands behind him, tied his ankles together, adjusted the rope about his neck and drew the cap over his face. While Bachtel [sic] was standing on the platform audibly praying, the Sherriff announced, at regular intervals, the number of minutes he had left to live, commencing at twenty, repeating every five minutes until the last five, when it was each minute. At the expiration of the last, he announced in a loud and distinct voice, "Christian Bachtel, your time is up, and may God almighty have mercy on your soul"; then, standing at the head of the stairway, he pulled the fulcrum that supported one side of the platform, and it fell with a crash that sent a shiver through the crowd.

His body was left hanging for thirty minutes before it was taken down and given to his friends. In the *Repository* article, Bachtle was described as "humble in the extreme" in his final days, resigning himself to his fate for killing his wife in cold blood.

2

AMELIA RICHARDSON

After enduring years of physical and mental abuse from her husband, Edward, Amelia Richardson shot and killed him with a Smith & Wesson revolver in the early morning hours of January 17, 1876, in their home above the grocery store he operated in Massillon at 24 West Main Street. The story shocked the small town because Edward was well known in the community, both as a grocer and as a city council member representing the Second Ward. In spite of a string of witnesses who testified on her behalf about abuse they had witnessed, her trial was not simply an open-and-shut case. Both sides called several medical experts to testify about the blood found at the scene, and a possible affair clouded the story, casting doubt on her innocence.

When police arrived on the scene that night, they found two victims. Edward was lying dead on the floor with a gunshot wound to his head. Amelia was found "in great excitement, with her throat cut and bleeding profusely, and a large amount of blood was found on her clothing, which consisted of a night dress and chemise, and had also a wound in her side," according to an article in the *Stark County Democrat* that appeared on January 20, a few days after the murder. The article described what Amelia told the police:

> The statement given by Mrs. Richardson is that she was asleep, was awakened by Richardson holding her down and endeavoring to cut her throat, that she spoke and said "for God's sake don't," and immediately

reached for her pistol, a seven shooting revolver which she had at the head of her bed, that he immediately seized the pistol and shot her, inflicting the wound in her side. She then wrenched the pistol from him and shot him. When the police entered the room they found the revolver with two empty chambers and five unexpended cartridges, and also the bloody razor…which corroborates Mrs. Richardson's statement.

In the same edition, the *Stark County Democrat* reported that Amelia's life was in danger after news broke of her husband's murder. "A large number of miners are in the city, and much excitement prevails. It is feared that the miners will undertake to lynch Mrs. Richardson. She is under arrest at the house where the murder was committed under strong guard. Richardson was very popular among the miners, having been one himself years ago. Influential citizens are trying to pacify the miners and induce them to go back to the mines. They have had little success up to this hour."

The next edition of the *Stark County Democrat*, published on January 27, included details about the coroner's jury, which was a group of men convened to assist a coroner in an inquest to determine the cause of death or to identify a victim. In this case, a coroner's jury was assembled because the coroner, Henry Altekruse Esq., was related to Edward Richardson by marriage. John G. Warwick, George Young, William Castleman, Henry Beatty, Edward Kachler and Kent Jarvis were selected. They heard witness testimony, similar to what would be heard in an actual trial.

Ezra Pietzcker, a nineteen-year-old who worked in Richardson's grocery store and boarded with the family, testified that he heard a gunshot during the night and was later woken by the Richardsons' daughter Ella, who told him that her father was shot and her mother's neck had been cut. On his way to the couple's bedroom, he met Amelia in the hallway, and he said that she said to him, "I've killed the old son of a b——h [*sic*]; he tried to kill me, but I got the upper hand of him." Pietzcker helped Amelia into another room, wrapped a towel around her bleeding neck and left to find a doctor and notify the police. He returned with Officers Thomas Seaman, George Miller and Turenne Goetz, who found both the gun and the bloody razor on the floor near Edward's body. Pietzcker was asked to identify the razor, and he said he "had seen it often" because Edward kept it on a shelf in the grocery store. He testified that the Friday before the murder, Edward was looking for his razor so he could shave, but it was not where he had left it. He asked Pietzcker if he had seen it. He had not. Edward said it was an old one anyway, and he assumed it had been stolen.

Pietzcker recounted for the coroner's jury that he had often "heard contentions and strife between them." Amelia had told him that she "wished they had parted twenty years ago, and was continually talking in the same strain. At supper the preceding Friday evening she had tried to persuade [the] witness to take sides with her, remarking that the deceased was 'nothing but a low-lived English pup, and that any how she would be his boss before long.'"

Pietzcker's testimony also included the fact that Edward had "often cautioned the witness not to repeat his wife's ill treatment, as he wanted all her abuse concealed from the public." He also recalled that when he first came to work for the Richardsons in September 1875, Amelia had told him that she had a pistol she kept "to fix him if he ever did anything to her." Pietzcker also said that in October he, his brother and Edward were all sickened after drinking liquor from the same bottle, which Amelia later admitted she had laced with croton oil, a plant-derived substance that causes diarrhea. The article concluded with the following: "A very important fact, not elicited before the Coroner's jury, but which was observed by four of the witnesses, was that when [the] deceased was found lying on the floor both his mouth and eyes were closed."

The prosecution's team included William A. Lynch (*pictured here*), William R. Day (*following page*) and Robert S. Shields of Canton and R.R. Folger of Massillon. While no photographs exist of Amelia or Edward Richardson, prominent attorneys are easily found in the historical record. *Courtesy of the McKinley Presidential Library & Museum.*

After a grand jury heard testimony from fifty-seven witnesses, Amelia was arraigned on February 22, 1876, and charged with first-degree murder. She pleaded not guilty. Her trial began on November 27, 1876, with Judge Joseph Frease presiding. The prosecution's team included Robert S. Shields, William A. Lynch and William R. Day of Canton and R.R. Folger of Massillon. The defense was led by John McSweeney of Wooster, Anson Pease and Augustus J. Ricks of Massillon and Colonel Seraphim Meyer of Canton. The following men served as jurors: Elias Wolcott, George M. Hershey, David Shanafelt, John J. Zaiser, Daniel Gibler, S.S. Bomberger, Frank E. McClain, Robert Van Horn, Joseph Putt, William Holabaugh, Jacob J. Yutzey and John Josephs. The *Repository* reported that the courtroom was "densely crowded" and there were "many ladies" present.

William R. Day. *Courtesy of the McKinley Presidential Library & Museum.*

The state's case focused on threatening statements Amelia had made to or in front of several witnesses and raised questions about her version of the events that night through expert medical testimony. The prosecution called Thomas Seaman, who was Massillon's marshal at the time of the murder, as its first witness. He testified that when he first saw Amelia, she was lying on a bed with a towel wrapped around her neck. She said, "Mr. Seaman, my husband tried to cut my throat with a razor, and I have shot him; is he dead?" Next, he went to the bedroom where the deceased was lying on the floor. He said that the first thing he noticed was the bed. A summary of his testimony was published in the December 1, 1876 edition of the *Repository*:

> *The clothes were turned back about two-thirds the length of the bed. The pillows were in their places, and there was no blood on them. On the south side of the bed, about four or six inches below the pillow, I noticed a blood stain. Richardson was lying on his back on the floor, his left foot at the edge of the bed, his body making an angle with the bed, his head being some distance from it. His hands were clean and spread out, and his legs were spread apart. His countenance was calm and he looked as if he might be sleeping. He had on no clothes but a white cotton shirt. There was no blood on it. There was a wound in his left temple, such as a No. 1 cartridge ball would make, and it looked burned and blackened. I examined Richardson and found him dead. A revolver with two chambers discharged was lying about 2 feet from his left hand, and a sharp razor was afterward handed to me by Ezra, which I think had been picked up by Mr. Miller. Razor was found in my absence and had blood stains on it. Saw blood on the carpet where R's head had lain. I then instructed the men with me to carefully observe the position of things in the room, as an inquest would be held and we would be summoned. We then lifted Richardson onto the bed, when in handling him his shirt became stained with the blood from my arm, which I had slipped under his neck. On the south of the bed, I noticed a comforter folded double under the sheet. The blood which I had observed below the pillow had not gone through to the mattress, though the comfort[er] was stained by it. I then charged the policemen to hold Mrs. Richardson in custody, and to allow no one to enter or leave the house while I went for the Coroner.*

Ezra Pietzcker took the stand on the second day of the trial. Most of his testimony was the same as what he had said at the inquest. In the trial, however, he said that he and the police had to look for the razor, which

Map of Massillon, 1870. When Amelia Richardson killed her husband, Massillon was a city with a population of about six thousand. Edward Richardson's grocery store was located at 24 West Main Street, and the couple lived on the second floor. *Library of Congress, Geography and Map Division.*

was found under a clean white handkerchief on the floor. He recounted the story Amelia had told him when he next saw her. "She took me by the hand and said: 'I was sleeping, when I felt someone trying to cut my throat; I threw up my hands and saw that it was R. I reached for my revolver. He saw me get it, and said he would use that, and he snatched the revolver and shot me before I could get out of bed. I grappled with him and got the revolver from him, and shot him. R was on one side of the bed and I was on the other. Oh Ezra! It's awful; just like that Cleveland thing." Amelia was likely referring to William Aiden, who had killed his wife, his stepdaughter Hattie and her friend with an axe on December 4, just two weeks before the Richardson murder took place. After years of quarreling, Aiden's wife had left him, but he had recently convinced her to return. After yet another argument, he killed her with an axe and then went to Mrs. Benton's home, where Hattie was staying, to kill her too. He attacked both women with the same axe. News of the triple murder was circulating throughout Ohio in the days before Richardson's death and was mentioned in the *Repository* one week before Amelia killed her husband. "There was an old trouble in the family," the article said. "Aiden is a brute, and will probably hang for his deeds."

Pietzcker testified that he heard Amelia tell Robert Warwick that they were about six or seven feet apart when she shot him. When asked if he had ever heard Amelia say anything about her husband, he replied that she had called him a "pot gut," saying that he had such a big belly he couldn't see his feet. She also said she hated him.

Next, Pietzcker was asked if he knew a man named Jacob Kryer (also spelled Cryer in some reports) and if he had ever discussed him with Amelia. He said he did know Kryer and had seen him walk and talk with Amelia Richardson once or twice. Kryer was a plasterer who had worked for Edward as a clerk before Pietzcker was hired. Then Pietzcker was asked if he remembered if Amelia had gone away. He said she had gone to Alliance by train with her sister and her youngest son. He added that Pietzcker was in the wagon with their daughter Ella and Mary Bowers, a servant girl, when she came home. "Kryer was at the depot," Pietzcker said. "He helped Mrs. R. into the wagon and kissed her. Upon separating, he told her to take care good of herself. She said she would, and that he should do the same. When we got home R. helped Mrs. R and Ella out of the wagon. He kissed Mrs. R. and shook hands with Charlie." The court adjourned in the middle of his testimony so the jury could visit the scene of the crime.

On Friday, Pietzcker's testimony concluded, and the state called Mary Bowers, the servant girl who worked for the Richardsons. She testified that she had seen Amelia with Kryer in all parts of the house almost every day, and sometimes they were alone. Further, she said that when Mr. Richardson was "up town," Kryer "most always went up to Mrs. Richardson's room." Ella, the couple's daughter, would yell upstairs from the downstairs hall, saying "Kryer, Pa's coming." Bowers said that Kryer would sometimes kiss Amelia when he left the dinner table, while Edward was in the grocery store. She also testified that she overheard a conversation between Amelia and Amelia's sister, who told her that she was "too intimate" with Kryer and people would talk. Amelia said he was her friend and she would treat him as such. Mary also overheard an argument between Amelia and Edward about Kryer. She said she and Ella helped pass notes between Amelia and Kryer. Upon cross-examination, Bowers said she never actually saw anything improper happen between them.

Several witnesses testified that they had seen Amelia and Kryer together around town. John O. Myers of Louisville testified that Amelia had checked into the St. Julian Hotel with a man, and they spent the night together in the same room. In the morning, they left in a buggy heading west, toward Canton. Three other witnesses said they saw the same thing.

Another witness called that day was Dr. A.W. Ridenour, who had done a postmortem examination with Dr. Reed the morning after the murder. Ridenour did not find any evidence of violence, save for the bullet wound in Edward Richardson's left temple. The victim's hair and the side of his face were bloody. When the physicians opened the skull, they found the bullet halfway through his brain. Richardson died instantly.

On the sixth day of the trial, Henry Altekruse testified that he told Amelia that he had seen her husband sitting in the grocery store crying. In the December 7, 1876 edition of the *Stark County Democrat*, Altekruse said he "told her that Richardson told me that he loved the very ground she walked on; she said if he did he had a very queer way of showing it." On the Friday before the murder, Amelia called Altekruse into her home. "She asked me what Richardson had been doing in Canton that morning; if he hadn't gone there to employ an attorney for a divorce case….I said I didn't know what he went there for." She told him Edward had offered her $6,000 for a divorce at one time but now only wanted to give her $3,000. Later testimony from Jacob Bachtel, the administrator of Edward's estate, estimated that at the time of his death his estate was valued at $28,000—$12,000 or $13,000 in real estate and the rest in personal property. Altekruse continued: "[I] said that Richardson had said to me that if she would only keep Kryer out of the house, all would be well; she said Kryer had always treated her right, and as long as he did so he was welcome to come to the house." Altekruse said he advised her to leave Kryer alone, not to be seen on the streets with him so often and to live with her husband "as she ought to do." On cross-examination, Altekruse denied that he had been asked to track Amelia's movements, and he said he never watched her.

The next witness was a Mrs. Ovington, who said that she saw Amelia about a week before the shooting. She said Amelia told her that Edward was in a bad mood and that if "things didn't turn for the better, either he or she would be missing some morning." Mrs. Ovington told her she shouldn't talk that way and said that Ella, who was also present, had said, "Ma, don't talk so loud he might hear you."

The next day, Robert Warwick testified that he had a conversation with Amelia about a separation from her husband but denied saying to anyone that it was "an outrage how he was treating her." It was his recollection that she would rather not go to court for a divorce, but she would if she could not get an adequate settlement from him outside of court.

Next, William Zink, a neighbor, testified that he and his wife were up with a sick child the night of the murder and heard a gunshot from the direction of the Richardsons' home around 1:30 a.m. He said he heard another shot about twenty minutes later from the same general location. He knew what time it was because he had "an old-fashioned clock" that chimed every half hour. He heard it chime just before the first shot, indicating it was 1:30 a.m. This would seem inconsistent with Amelia's version of what happened that night. Throughout the prosecution's case, witnesses repeatedly testified that Amelia had told them the same story:

Dr. Theodore G. Wormley and his wife were the guests of Robert S. Shields (*pictured*) at his home at 922 West Tuscarawas Street during Amelia's trial. Shields was one of the prosecuting attorneys. *Courtesy of the McKinley Presidential Library & Museum.*

she was sleeping and felt someone trying to cut her throat, she pushed him away, grabbed the revolver she kept by her bed, he grabbed it from her and shot her, she wrestled it back and shot him. Yet Mr. and Mrs. Zink testified that they had heard two gunshots approximately twenty minutes apart. After Zink's testimony, the prosecution's case shifted toward medical evidence the state hoped would show that the Amelia's wounds were not inflicted in the manner in which she had told witnesses.

The seventh day of the trial would be a historical first for Stark County. Several witnesses who saw the initial crime scene testified that they saw a bloodstain near the pillow on the bed. Theodore G. Wormley—a physician, analytical chemist and professor of microchemistry and toxicology at Starling Medical College in Columbus—took the stand. In 1867, he wrote an eight-hundred-page book titled *The Micro-chemistry of Poisons*, which became a standard text when medical science and court proceedings intersected. For seven years preceding the trial, Dr. Wormley's work had focused on the analysis of blood. He had been called as an expert witness many times, and he was asked to testify in this case "to show which side of the blood-stained sheet the blood was first received upon."

The *Stark County Democrat*'s initial coverage of this significant testimony is disappointing, saying only: "The Professor's explanations were of a thoroughly scientific nature, and he was requested to remain in the city, as his services might be further desired." The *Repository* reported more details regarding Dr. Wormley's testimony:

> *Here the sheet was produced that was found on Richardson's bed the morning of his death and identified as the one brought to Dr. Wormley's laboratory at Columbus on last Saturday, by Mr. Day. The question involved was, as to which side of the sheet the blood producing the spot frequently referred to before as being seen near the pillow on the south side of the bed, was received. The Dr. made evidence that he had carefully examined the spot on the sheet by aid of the microscope, and that, in the light of numerous results obtained by him in bringing cotton textures into apposition with fresh blood, gave it as his judgement that the blood on the sheet had been applied on the clotted side. Here Mr. Day, one of the attorneys for the state, explained the manner in which the sheet had been found on the bed the morning of the tragedy, and showed to the jury that the clotted blood was found on the under side of the sheet. The Dr. said that it was possible to have applied the blood to the under side of the sheet by bringing it into contact with or dipping it in blood; he did not regard it as at all probable that the blood*

should have percolated through the sheet and coagulated on the under side. The Dr. was requested to produce his microscope, and the blood spot was viewed through it by the counsel and jury; the Dr. testified that science had furnished no test by which the blood of one person could be distinguished from that of another, and that it would not be possible by examination to ascertain whether the blood found on the carpet and that found on the sheet belonged to the same or different persons.

Most of the afternoon was devoted to Dr. Wormley's testimony and cross-examination, which included detailed questioning on scientific theories on the "composition and properties of blood." According to the *Repository*, Dr. Wormley's testimony was "clear and masterly." Local physician Dr. Lorenzo M. Whiting was called to the stand next, and he agreed with Dr. Wormley's testimony, adding that "the skin on the side of a woman who had borne children is very flexible," which the prosecution hoped would show that Amelia could have pulled her own skin out at her waist and shot through it herself.

The first witness called the next day, the eighth day of the trial, was Dr. Auren W. Whiting, Dr. Lorenzo Whiting's brother. He shared with the court his observations regarding Amelia's injuries. He characterized the cuts on her neck as "so slight that it seemed as if they had been cut carefully; would require more care to cut a slight wound then a deeper one; wounds were just through the skin," according to the *Repository*. Dr. Whiting's testimony seemed to suggest that Amelia inflicted the cuts on her neck herself. He had also examined her gunshot wound, which he characterized as "superficial." He noted that the skin on her side was "very flexible and susceptible of being grasped up in the hand." He suggested that the entrance and exit of the bullet were "shortened some way, and the skin twisted or wrinkled," which seemed to suggest that her skin was pulled away from her body and shot through. Dr. Whiting also testified that he "never saw a person killed instantly but what the eyes were open." Edward's eyes were closed when witnesses first entered the crime scene. The doctor admitted, however, that he had never seen a murder victim whom he knew was killed while asleep. Later that day, Dr. George Scott also testified that "if the eyes of a person instantaneously killed were found closed it would indicate the fact that the eyes were closed at the time of death." Several other doctors were called to the stand, corroborated the expert blood testimony and said that the eyes of a murder victim would remain as they were at the moment he or she was killed.

Next, the prosecution called Mary Baxter to the stand. She was present at the home of Henry Altekruse on Thanksgiving night in 1875 and had heard an exchange between Mr. and Mrs. Richardson. "I was sitting on a lounge near the window," the *Repository* reported. "Saw Mrs. R. standing at the window outside; heard her say, 'Is this where I find you? I want you to come right out here; this is a nice place; you have no business to be here when I am not here'; she called him a bloody hearted son of a b———h [*sic*], and said when he came home she would pull every hair out of his head; R had a glass of wine in his hand, and I heard her say she wished she was in there, she would put something in the wine that he never would drink any more; she had something in her hand and shook it and said, 'Here's something that will not let you go another place without me.' Couldn't say what it was; R walked up to the window and said: 'I am here with my friends, Mrs. R, independent of you.' Mrs. Altekruse told her to come in, that she was welcome; she told her she didn't want any fuss at her house."

The crowd continued to grow with each day of the case. Before reporting on the ninth through the twelfth days of the trial, the *Stark County Democrat* noted, "The murder case still goes on with daily increasing attendance, if such a thing is possible. The seats in the auditorium and gallery, the aisles, the bar, and even the steps leading to the Judge's bench, are occupied by spectators—men, women and children. Some come from a genuine desire to hear and follow the case through; but others, merely out of curiosity to see the accused."

The prosecution rested its case in the afternoon of the ninth day of the trial. It was now the defense team's turn to build its case for murder by self-defense, using a string of witness testimony to show that Amelia had suffered several years of mental and physical abuse at the hands of her husband. The first witness called was Mrs. A. Howell, who had lived with the Richardsons for six months in 1869. She said it was common for Edward to call her names such a "d—n Dutch s—n of a b—h" at least five or six times a week. She said Amelia never said anything to her husband but would "go off and cry about it." Mrs. Howell said she visited in July 1875 and found Amelia's face "dreadfully bruised swollen, her eyes blood-shot, and a lump the size of a hickory nut on the right side of her forehead; her face was purple; she was in bed." She said she would not have recognized her if she had seen her out somewhere. Next, Louis Stilkey testified that two weeks before Thanksgiving, he entered Edward's grocery store to get change for a two dollar bill. On his way to the money drawer, Edward passed Amelia, and Stilkey heard him say, "I'll be d—d,

I'll cut that woman's throat yet." He said he didn't know whether he meant Mrs. R or not, but there was no one else in the store at the time. The final witness of the day was James A. Hackett, who owned a furniture store across the alley from the Richardsons' home. He said that he had seen Edward several times the day of the murder, and he acted very strangely. He had been drinking, and "his eyes were wild—staring at me—gazed at me." Hackett said his behavior was unusual because he was "not in the habit of coming into my store."

The next day, on the tenth day of the trial, Henry Cramer testified that while he was boarding with the Richardsons and employed as a clerk in the grocery store, he heard Edward many times call Amelia a "red headed b—h," a "wh—re," and a "G—d d—n b—h." Cramer said he heard this happen sometimes every day for a while, then not for a week or two. Amelia never said a word back to Edward. Cramer recalled a time when she "had her nose nearly cut off." Although he did not see it happen, when he returned home one Sunday morning, he found her in bed, "with a deep cut in the bridge of her hose; her eyes were black and there was a lump the size of a marble on her forehead." Cramer noted that when he walked into the house, Edward had said to him, "So, you came in to see about the fuss, did you?" Another time Cramer testified that he saw Edward "hit her on the face and hand, and scratched her face." Cramer jumped between them to separate them, and he "struck at her three times across my shoulder." Her face was bleeding. He also testified that while working in the grocery store, he heard Edward say, "I'll cut her d—d heart out."

Next, William J. Wheeler testified that in October 1875 he went into the grocery store to get a glass of beer and saw Edward and Amelia quarreling. She left the room, and Edward said, "I'll soon be done with you, you d—d red-headed b—h." Wheeler said, "What's that, Ed?" as he received his beer. And Richardson said, "Nothing, only that d—d b—h of a woman of mine; I'll get rid of her some day."

Then George Archer was called to the stand. He said about two years prior to the murder, he went into the grocery to get some sugar. As Edward was weighing it, Amelia came in and said, "Mr. Archer, look at my eyes and face, just see how Ed has pounded me up.…[She] showed me her eyes and throat; her throat and one of her wrists [was] scratched; I then went to pay R. for sugar, and as I laid down my money, he said, 'By Jesus'; his manner seemed mad; Mrs. R's eyes were black, under the eyes; also marks on her nose and think there was a scratch also on one of her cheeks; throat

CANTONS FAMILY ALBUM

By GRETCHEN PUTNAM.

IT WAS 71 years ago that this little girl in hoop skirts and hair in long curls posed for her picture.

The tiny picture, despite the years, is in splendid condition and the prized possession of her daughter.

As Ella Richardson, she lived in Massillon with her parents and was nine years old when the picture was taken. Were she living today she would be 80 years old.

When she grew to womanhood she became the bride of J. A. Heingartner a Canton wall paper merchant of the firm Hoeland & Heingartner.

Mrs. Heingartner, above, died four years ago. Her daughter, Mrs. Ed Yant, and one son, Edward Richeimer reside in Canton, and another son, Frank Richeimer lives in Chicago. Mr. Heingartner passed on a number of years ago.

This is the only known image of Ella Richardson. It was taken approximately ten years prior to her father's death on January 17, 1876. It was reprinted in the *Repository* on November 20, 1937, with no mention of the scandal that had rocked her family. *Courtesy of the* Repository.

scratched two or three places; she looked pretty hard, don't know if she had been crying, but she looked rough; R. made no explanation except that oath."

Next, the couple's nineteen-year-old daughter, Ella, testified about the abuse she witnessed for most of her young life. She said it had been happening as far back as she could remember. Three or four years earlier, around the Fourth of July, she heard her father swearing at her mother.

She went in the grocery and told him not to drink; this was in the morning right after breakfast; she said, "Pa, don't drink so much," he said, "I'll take as much as I g—d d—d please, independent of you"; he had been drinking two or three Sundays before that, this was Sunday morning; heard this from kitchen; Ma hollowed and I ran in; saw her face was bleeding; she was calling me; ran to help her; found them in hall; and Pa was striking her with his fist; she was facing south and he north, striking her with both fists; ran between to separate them: Pa struck about three times after I ran between then; struck over my shoulder; begged and said "O Pa, don't strike her"; he pushed me away and went in grocery swearing; then noticed Ma's face was bleeding; then coaxed her to come in room with me; she commenced to cry then; I washed her face off; it was awful bloody; don't know how deep or how bad her nose was cut; awful cut I know; seen something in his hand, but couldn't see what it was; it was more like a weight than anything; she had a mark on her forehead; saw that after we got in room; mark on her forehead large as a hickory nut; Ma was in bed after that about three weeks; didn't know anything for over a week; before this, from the time I was able to know anything, it was nothing but swearing from father to her; remember coffee pot transaction when young; remember tea kettle thrown at her, and she taking me upstairs crying; Pa upset table this same time; got tea kettle off of stove; without mentioning particular times heard him call her a "G—d d—d red headed b—h," "G—d d—d Dutch b—h," "idiot," and a "fool," "G—d Dutch wh—re"; heard such things as far as I can remember; said before me and little Charlie; Ma would sometimes say, "don't talk so, Pa, before the children," she said "she was Dutch before she was married and what did he take her for," in answer to him calling her Dutch; she also said, "her hair was red before he married her;" couldn't pretend to get the number of times heard these things in my life.

Ella also told the court what she witnessed on the day Cramer broke up the fight between her parents:

He went up and struck Ma; first on the head with his fist; that was in room; he fought with her til they got in the kitchen, and Henry and I ran between them; he was striking her all the way out to the kitchen; she tried to defend herself; tried to push him away; held her hands straight out and dodged head from blows; when we ran between he walked off to the grocery, swearing; Ma's face was bleeding right side of forehead; wound on her hand also, on knuckle; mark on her knuckle yet; her face was black and blue after; Kramer and I stood in front door, I think in July, '75, between 7 and 8 o'clock in the evening; Pa came first to pump in front of house and then walked around the house; came to door; Ma and Charlie were sitting on lounge in sitting room and right at door; as soon as I heard Pa coming Henry started away, and Pa caught me by the arm and dragged me to the other end of the room, and kicked me in the side; Ma was still on the lounge, and said, "That's no way to correct a child"; he said, "She should mind her own G—d d—d businesses, he was not doing anything to her"; she replied, "I'll defend my children as long as I live, or there's a bit of blood in my body"; he said, "you will, G—d d—n you," and struck her several times; no less than seven or eight times; commenced in sitting room and continued to dining room, she struggling till they got that far....Charlie pleaded for Pa to stop hitting Ma; he said, "Oh, Pa, please don't hit Ma;" think Charlie took him by coat; I was hollowing murder, and saw no one was coming, and then I called Kryer; Kryer was up stairs in bed, with a sore foot, hardly able to stand; he came down as Pa was coming toward me, calling me names, and Kryer slipped up and said, "Mr. Richardson, that's your daughter and wife"; Pa said: "G—d d—m you Dutch b—hs of wh—res to h—l"; soon as Pa said that he went into the grocery, swearing; found Ma had a lump on her forehead, nose and mouth bleeding; cut on lower lip made mouth bleed; I washed the blood and then shut up sitting room and then went up stairs; Ma's face was marked and black and blue and awfully swollen; she was sick about four weeks;' waited on her, and toward last Aunt Wonders helped; Ma was so low at one time that she didn't know anybody; she was out of her mind; I said, "Pa, Ma's awful low, won't you come up and see her?" He said, "he didn't believe a d—n word that she was sick, she was just pretending."

Kryer quit six or seven weeks after this incident. Ella also testified that she did not hear her mother say she "killed the s—n of a b—h" to Pietzcker as he had claimed. She said after his testimony at the inquest came out in the paper, she confronted him and asked him how he could lie about that. At first, he denied that he said it, but when Ella took the newspaper out of her pocket and read it to him, he turned and left without saying a word. Ella's testimony continued on the eleventh day of the trial, where she said she never told her mother not to speak so loud or he would hear her, as Mrs. Ovington had testified. The *Stark County Democrat* noted that the "cross examination was long and searching, but nothing new of importance was elicited." The *Repository* mentioned that under cross-examination, Ella had said that "Pa at times was very kind; made abundant provisions for the family; and furnished the house nicely." Later in the trial, Ella's thirteen-year-old brother, Charlie, testified about the "cruel treatment" he witnessed from his father toward his mother. His specific testimony was not reported.

The same day, Amelia's sister Christiana Morganthalter testified about the incident when her nose was cut. "Her face was very much swollen," the *Repository* said, "and there was a large gash across the nose; she was out of her head and did not know me; she appeared frightened and said R. was coming after her with an ax; I remained until evening; I talked with R. about the matter after I saw her and asked what was the cause of the trouble; he said, 'She drives away my customers that I make money on'; I said I would not sell whisky to any one who would make trouble in my family; he said he would sell to any body who had money; I coaxed him to go up and see Mrs. R; he went up and stood at the door and said nothing." Further, she testified that she ran into Edward one night after Amelia had returned from her trip to Alliance. She said Edward said to her, "I'm glad I am a week older, I'd have shot them both." When she said, "Oh, no, you couldn't have done that," he replied, "Yes, they would both be dead now. That was my intention."

Amelia's older sister Fredericka Wonders testified briefly, and then Christiana Morganthalter was recalled to the stand. Attorney Day asked her if she had been at Altekruse's home the previous week. "I was," she said. He continued, "While there, did you not say that you knew Mrs. Richardson was guilty, but she had suffered enough in jail, and as Ed is dead now, we should do all we could to clear her?" Christiana responded, "Never! Never! Never!"

Before Dr. Lew Slusser testified about the Amelia's wounds, the judge, jury, attorneys and medical experts examined, in private, the scars on

Three of Amelia's family members testified on her behalf, including her brother Leonard Bammerlin (*right*); her mother, Mary Bammerlin (*opposite, left*); and her father, Charles Bammerlin (*opposite, right*). Courtesy of the Massillon Museum.

her neck and side. Dr. Slusser's testimony differed from the prosecution's expert witnesses, saying that he believed the wound on her side was caused by a gunshot from a distance, since there was no evidence of powder marks on her body or clothing that night. He said that he found the flesh on her side "rather tense and not easily gathered up" as the other doctors had testified. He also said that he would not expect much blood to flow from the type of gunshot wound in Edward's head, and he "could not give any satisfactory evidence on the condition of a person's eyes in the case of instant death."

On the twelfth day of the trial, Wonders returned to the stand. She testified that she had spoken to Edward about how badly he was treating his wife about a year before the murder, and he had agreed that he would try to do better. Next, Jonathan O. Myers testified that Edward had taken a train to Alliance, hoping to find his wife with Kryer. When he returned for his buggy later that evening, he said he had not found them, but added that "if he had found them at the train he would have shot them both." Their nephew Layfayette Wonders testified that he also heard Edward say the same thing.

Amelia's brother Leonard Bammerlin was the last witness of the day. He testified that on the Thursday before the murder, Amelia had asked him to come to their house to help her "settle the trouble" between her and her

husband. Bammerlin went to Edward and said, "How shall I commence? Shall I make peace or arrange a divorce?" He said Edward told him, "There ain't a d—d bit of use to make up in peace. Tell her I'll give her $3000, and that's all." Bammerlin took this message to his sister, and while they were talking, Edward came into the room with a piece of paper in his hand, and said, "Thank fortune, I'm ahead of you this time. Here's a letter from McSweeney: 'Your telegram is received. I will be at your service at any call. John McSweeney.'" McSweeney was one of Amelia's defense lawyers, but she had apparently approached him to be her divorce attorney prior to the murder.

On the thirteenth day of the trial, the defense called both of Amelia's parents to testify. Her father, Charles Bammerlin, who was eighty-four at the time, testified that he had spoken to his son-in-law about how he treated his daughter, "but it never amounted to anything." Her mother, Mary, said she was at the house when Amelia's nose was cut. She corroborated previous testimony that Amelia was "out of her head" after the incident for at least a week.

Next, the defense rolled out a series of medical experts who disagreed with what the prosecution's experts had said. Dr. Bennett of Cleveland was the chair of principles of medicine at Western Reserve College and had been a practicing physician for twenty-six years, including sixteen years in

Michigan and in the military. During his time in the army, he said he had "daily opportunities" to observe the aftereffects of gunshot wounds. He refuted Dr. Wormley's testimony: "I have examined the sheet, and though I would not say that I can state positively which side of the sheet received the blood, in my judgement it was applied in the side marked by the absence of clot." He also said there is no "uniform or arbitrary rule" about whether a murder victim's eyes would be open or closed when killed instantly, and he had seen examples of both.

Next, Dr. Thayer, a surgeon and chair of surgery and jurisprudence at the Cleveland Medical College, took the stand. He had also served in the army, which afforded him a great deal of experience with gunshot wounds. He said that "blood may pass through several thicknesses of fabric before it clots." He agreed with Dr. Bennett, saying the blood was received on the side of the sheet that was not clotted. After examining Amelia's wounds, Dr. Thayer concluded they were homicidal, not suicidal, in nature. He said, "I have examined the wounds in Mrs. Richardson's side; she could not have drawn up the flesh so as to shoot herself, as there is not enough space between the wounds to take hold without shooting her fingers." He also testified that most suicide victims cut their throats from left to right, and her wounds were located more to the right than to the left, which seemed to indicate that she had not inflicted them herself.

Dr. Firestone, the chair of diseases of women at the University of Wooster, was the next witness. He said, "I have had considerable experience with blood. When warm and fresh it will pass through fabrics and coagulate where it rests; motion retards coagulation; in bandages of several thicknesses the clot is found on the fold farthest from the wound." He agreed with the previous two medical witnesses who believed the blood was received on the unclotted side of the sheet. In his opinion, it was "highly improbable" that the gunshot wound on Amelia's side was self-inflicted.

The final witness of the day, Dr. X.C. Scott of Western Reserve University in Cleveland, "substantially corroborated" the previous three medical expert witnesses. But in cross-examination, the state "produced an experiment, in which fresh blood had been allowed to run from a man's arm unto a muslin fabric underlined with calico, filled with cotton batting, similar to sheet and comforters in the Richardson case, in which the clot was formed on the top or receiving side."

On the fourteenth day of the trial, the defense called yet another medical expert, Dr. R.U. Piper, author of the book *Operative Surgery*

Illustrated, who specialized in studying blood. He testified that different blood coagulates at different rates, citing a recent experiment he had conducted with fresh blood from two different animals. One coagulated instantly, and the other "is yet liquid." He took blood from Amelia's arm and compared it under a microscope to the blood on the sheet, and "the corpuscles* correspond exactly." He also examined the blood on the carpet, which came from underneath Edward, and said "if the blood on the sheet and on the carpet flowed the same night they are not from the same person."

All of the testimony regarding blood was a novelty in Canton in 1876. On December 21, the *Stark County Democrat* published this tongue-in-cheek report, separate from any coverage of the trial itself:

> *Our people, those at least who attended the Richardson trial last week, should be familiar with the composition of the blood and its varied properties. There was such an elucidation by experts of serum, and fibrin and albumen, and coagulum and corpuscles and the like; and then the microscope was introduced, and each juror was requested to take a peep to determine on which side of the fabric the fluid was first received in addition to which much light was thrown upon the differential properties of human blood, and that of other mammals, and how to distinguish it from the blood of birds and fishes. Hereafter should a dispute arise in our community on the subject of blood, we would recommend as a referee any one of the jurors of this trial. If he is unable to settle the question, it would be useless to make further effort.*

On the fifteenth day of the trial, the defense rested its case. The prosecution called witnesses who testified that Edward was sober on the day of the murder, including a "colored" barber in Massillon named Ishmael Palmer. Next they called Elizabeth Craig, who was present the day that Amelia's nose was injured. She said Amelia had gone into the grocery store looking for a fight, but Edward was not interested in arguing. As he was trying to get her out the door, "she turned and struck her nose against the doorway, she turned to me and said, 'Have I hurt my nose much?'" The last witness of the day was Washington Miller, who had been on the grand jury that indicted Amelia. He testified that Ella had not shared as many details about the arguments between her parents then as she did in the present trial.

---

* The word *corpuscle* refers to red or white blood cells today.

On the final day of the trial, the state recalled blood expert Dr. Wormley, who refuted Dr. Piper's testimony regarding corpuscles in the blood sample from the stain on the sheet. He said that from the evidence presented, one could not say that the two groups of corpuscles were "from the same individual, or even from the same species." He said that one could only say that "certain blood was consistent with human blood, not that it *is* human blood." Dr. Auren Whiting and Dr. Lorenzo Whiting were also recalled to refute parts of the testimony of the opposing side's medical experts. Dr. A.W. Whiting insisted that the source of blood could not be determined, and Dr. L.M. Whiting said he has seen suicide victims cut themselves directly across the neck.

In its coverage of the trial, the *Cincinnati Enquirer* noted that McSweeney's closing argument on Amelia's behalf was powerful, although no transcript of it exists. "The last appeal for the prisoner and her children, a little boy and daughter, just blooming into womanhood, was most touchingly eloquent and pathetic, bringing tears to many eyes."

With both sides finished presenting their cases, it was now the up to the jury to decide if Amelia was guilty of murder, and if so, in what degree. In his instructions to the jury, Judge Frease explained the differences between first-degree murder, second-degree murder and manslaughter. According to an act passed by the General Assembly of the State of Ohio on March 1, 1835, first-degree murder was defined as murder committed deliberately and with premeditated malice. Second-degree murder was murder committed "purposely and maliciously, but without premeditation and deliberation." To convict someone of manslaughter meant that he or she killed someone "without malice, either upon a sudden quarrel or unintentionally." Although Amelia had been charged with first-degree murder, the jury could choose to find her guilty of the lesser crimes of second-degree murder or manslaughter.

Further, Judge Frease defined the terms *premeditated* and *deliberate* for the jury:

> Premeditated *means thought of, designed or contemplated before the actual commission of the act, and not originally conceived at the very moment of the deed.*
>
> Deliberate *means turned over in the mind, weighed and considered so as to form a settled and sedate purpose. To constitute deliberation, she must by reflection have understood what she intended to do, and have designed to do it in order to harm.*

Judge Frease cautioned the jury that in order to find Amelia guilty of murder, they needed to consider whether the testimony heard during the trial established her guilt "beyond a reasonable doubt," which he defined as "an honest uncertainty existing in the mind of an honest, impartial, reasonable man, after a full and careful consideration of all the evidence, with a desire to ascertain the truth." He told them they must consider the credibility of each witness in evaluating what really happened. If they agreed with the notion that Edward assaulted her first, cutting her throat with a razor and shooting her in the side, and she shot him in the heat of the moment, but not in self-defense, then they needed to find her guilty of manslaughter. If they believed that she acted in self-defense, she should be acquitted. Judge Frease explained the right of self-defense, as recognized by the State of Ohio: "That homicide is justifiable on the ground of self defence [sic], where the slayer, in the careful and proper use of his faculties, in good faith believes, and has reasonable grounds to believe, that he is in imminent danger of death or great bodily harm, and that his only means of escape will be by taking the life of his assailant, although in fact, he is mistaken as to the existence or imminence of the danger."

Judge Frease cautioned the jury about testimony that included conversations either with the deceased, the accused, or both, and also sometimes with the witnesses, because the "meaning and intention of a person in a conversation often depends upon gesture, mode of expression, or peculiar attending circumstances, known perhaps but to few present. A conversation may not be fully heard by the witness, it may be imperfectly recollected, or inaccurately repeated, with the omission or addition of a single word, or the substitution of the language of the witness under color of bias or excitement, for the words actually used might change the sense of an entire conversation." He noted the "irreconcilable contradictions" that arose from the conflicting testimony of witnesses. He also warned them that their decision should be based exclusively on the testimony given in court and should in no way be influenced by public opinion.

The jury was dismissed at 7:00 p.m. on Saturday evening. They deliberated all night, reaching a verdict at 8:00 a.m. on Sunday, which was also Christmas Eve. The courthouse bell rang, alerting the people of Canton that the jury had reached a conclusion. The *Stark County Democrat* noted, "Although but comparatively few people are usually stirring abroad at this hour on Sabbath morning, a large number assembled at the ringing of the bell, and the court room was soon fairly filled." After the judge, the attorneys and the jurors were seated, Amelia was brought into the courtroom. Jury foreman Elias Wallcut read the following: "We the Jury impaneled and sworn to well and truly try, and true deliverance make between the State of Ohio and the prisoner at the bar, Amelia Richardson, do find the defendant guilty of manslaughter, and not guilty of murder in the first or second degrees, as charged in the indictment." Amelia was shocked. She and her attorneys believed that they had successfully built a case for self-defense and no doubt expected her to be found not guilty of any charges.

In January, Amelia's attorneys petitioned the court for a new trial, which Judge Frease denied, claiming that one of the jurors had an "opinion previous to the trial" and also the discovery of new evidence, according to the *Stark County Democrat*. At sentencing, Judge Frease asked Amelia if she had anything to say, and she said "she was not guilty of any crime, but simply committed an act of self defense, when she broke completely down and sank into her chair sobbing." Her attorneys asked the court to make her sentence as light as possible. Judge Frease sentenced her to three years in the Ohio penitentiary. "Mrs. Richardson was greatly agitated and sobbed bitterly on hearing the sentence pronounced."

Soon after her conviction, Amelia's attorneys applied for a pardon to Governor Thomas L. Young, who had replaced Rutherford B. Hayes when Hayes was elected president in 1875. Young refused to pardon her and expressed concern about the light sentence she had received. Amelia eventually received her pardon from Governor Richard M. Bishop on March 15, 1878, "in consideration of the probability of the act being done in self-defense and under provocation of gross maltreatment at the time," according to the *Annual Reports for 1878 Made to the Sixty-Third General Assembly of the State of Ohio*. She was immediately released and returned to her home in Massillon.

In November 1878, Amelia found herself in a civil suit brought against her by the state to recover the costs of her murder trial, which was over $2,000. Judge Meyer ruled in her favor after her attorney submitted her pardon. The *Repository*'s opinion about the governor's "liberal pardoning prerogative" was abundantly clear, noting that no county saw as many pardons to convicted criminals as Stark had seen:

> *We will not attempt a discussion of the merits of the Richardson matter, as the public have long since made up their verdict as to the guilt or innocence of the defendant, in that memorable case. But it certainly seems sufficient that a person on whose head rested such a dark suspicion*

Amelia died in 1933, almost sixty years after she killed her husband. She is buried alongside him, with a joint stone, in Massillon City Cemetery. *Author's photo.*

of guilt, should have been pardoned and returned to her home and to the enjoyment of liberty, without remitting the costs of her prosecution, the payment of which would, indeed, have been a small penalty for the terrible crime which she was charged withal.

A feeling of intense indignation is felt over the action of the Governor, and if he desires to retain even the few party followers which he has in Stark County, he must be made to feel that her taxpayers do not care to incur the heavy court expenses under which they are groaning, to allow him to exercise, without discrimination, a prerogative whose indiscreet use has been the only notable feature of his feeble administration.

Amelia lived to be ninety-six years old. Her name stayed out of the newspapers for the rest of her life, except when her trial was recounted in columns that looked back "On This Day" twenty-five or fifty years ago. On March 2, 1887, the *Repository* reported that Charles and Ella moved to Chicago, and Amelia is listed in the census in or around Chicago in

1910, 1920 and 1930. Between 1930 and 1933, she returned to Canton to live with Ella, who had moved back sometime earlier, at 321 Walnut Street SE. She died on August 6, 1933, two months after Ella. Amelia's obituary did not hint at the dramatic events that occurred in the 1870s. She is buried alongside her husband, with a joint stone, in Massillon City Cemetery.

3

TRIPLE HANGING

The triple hanging in 1880 of three teenage boys—Gustave Ohr, George Mann and John Sammet (also spelled Sammett)—for two separate murders was only the second execution in Canton's history and a spectacle unlike anything ever seen in the city. Victor L. Streib wrote the following in an article titled "Capital Punishment of Children in Ohio" in the *Akron Law Review*: "The public hanging of Mann and Ohr, along with John Sammet, was the occasion for a community-wide extravaganza. People came to the small town of Canton in eastern Ohio by excursion train from as far away as Chicago and Pittsburgh to witness the event. A circus was part of the extravaganza and the night before the hangings included much music, cannon firing, speech making and similar merriment." Indeed, the triple hanging was listed in the "Coming Events" column of the June 14, 1880 edition of the *Repository*, blithely sandwiched between listings for the Democratic National Convention and Akron's Sangerfest.

The tragic story began on June 27, 1879. Gustave Ohr, sixteen, and George Mann, nineteen or twenty, were traveling from Chicago with an older man named John Wattmaugh (also spelled Whatmaugh in some reports), who was on his way home to Philadelphia after an unsuccessful trip west to find work. He fixed looms and other weaving machinery and had hoped to find work in Illinois where he had friends. He was low on cash, so he was walking along the railroad tracks and hitching a ride on freight trains when he could. Along the way he met Mann, and later Ohr, who were also traveling east. The trio stopped near Alliance and

Left: George Mann, nineteen or twenty, was born in England and came to the United States with his family when he was very young. He did not get along with his stepmother back in Kansas, so he was traveling east to New York City to meet up with his brother.

Right: Gustave Adolphus Ohr was born in Bavaria and, like Mann, emigrated with his family at an early age. He blamed "flashy literature" for his downfall. He wanted to go on an adventure, like some of his favorite characters. He said, "I didn't have to tramp, but I went just because I wanted some fun." *Images reprinted from* The Criminal Classes, Causes and Cures *by Daniel Right Miller (1903)*.

purchased some food for breakfast, which they ate in the woods in the northeast part of the city.

Ohr and Mann hatched a plan earlier to rob their traveling companion and then flee. When Wattmaugh fell asleep, the boys "struck him over the head with a railroad coupling pin, took his money, shoes, and some articles of personal clothing," according to the chapter "History of the Bench and Bar of Stark County, Ohio" by James H. Robertson Esq. in the book *Bench and Bar of Northern Ohio*. Wattmaugh managed to stagger to a nearby house, his head "horribly crushed and beaten," and uttered a few words about what had happened to him. He soon fell unconscious and died. Witnesses had seen the three of them enter the woods and the two boys exit alone, so they were immediately the primary suspects. Marshal Kingsbury "started east in a buggy," according to the December 4, 1879 edition of the *Stark County*

Democrat, "and arrived at the first station before they did." The boys were arrested and sent to jail in Alliance.

Sheriff Rauch allowed a reporter from the *Repository* to interview Ohr and Mann on June 29, giving Canton its first glimpse of the accused. Calling their crime "cold blooded, broad daylight butchery," the reporter described the victim's hair as "whitened with the frosts of many winters." Wattmaugh had a total of five dollars and a watch in his possession, for which he was killed. "Think of it," the reporter said, "the old man had only a few moments before the fatal blow was struck, shared his scanty meal of cheese and crackers" with the boys. Initially, Ohr admitted to killing Wattmaugh, although he said the boys had planned the robbery together.

The article described each boy's life up until the crime. Gustavus Adolphus Ohr was born in Bavaria, Germany, and emigrated with his family when he was one year old. His father had died when he was still a child, and his mother remarried and was living in Chicago. Ohr had one brother who was living in New York City at the time of the murder. The *Repository* described Ohr as "quite intelligent," noting that he could read and write in both English and German and was a cigarmaker by trade. He said he "fell in" with Mann and Wattmaugh at Fort Wayne, two days before the murder. Ohr said he knew how much money Wattmaugh had, but he did not intend to kill him, just stun him, so he could rob him more easily. "When asked why it was necessary to inflict so many blows to accomplish his purpose, [he] said that the old gentleman resisted after the first blow and the others followed to quiet him." Ohr stole Wattmaugh's clothes and was wearing them when he was arrested. The article continued:

> *The boy does not look like one that could commit such an act, but his seeming ignorance of the enormity of the crime he has committed is strange. In reply to his question as to what I thought would be the final result, I told him that to put the affair in the best light possible, he had a terrible job on his hands, to which he replied, that he was prepared to die, but he never intended to kill the old man. He can not imagine what made him think of doing such a thing, but it is all over and can not be helped now.*

Next, the article focused on George William Mann, who was born in England and also emigrated with his family when he was young. He did not know his exact age and told the reporter he was around nineteen or twenty. His mother died when he was three, and his father remarried and was living in Kansas. He did not get along with his stepmother, so he was traveling to

New York City to meet up with his brother who was a barber. Mann had worked on the family farm for most of his life and did not learn a trade, although he had briefly worked in a tailor shop.

Mann said he had met up with Wattmaugh about two weeks prior to the murder in Decatur, Illinois. He told the reporter that Ohr had "wanted him to help but he could not do it, and had nothing to do with the killing." He said he had been lying next to Wattmaugh on the ground when he saw Ohr hit him the first time and "immediately after the first blow started to run away." He said he "heard the old man call for his friends. He undoubtedly thinking that he had been attacked by strangers; that after running a short distance he became faint and weak, he sat down, and soon after Ohr came up and gave him the watch and $2.50 in a pocket book, and told him to come on and keep his mouth shut." Mann and Ohr traveled together until they were caught by the marshal of Alliance. Mann was carrying the red bundle witnesses saw in Wattmaugh's possession, and Ohr was wearing the deceased's hat, pants and vest.

Mann said he did not know why he took the watch and money from Ohr, and he admitted that it was wrong for him to have done so. He insisted that he had nothing to do with the murder, and he intended to prove that he would never do such a thing through character witnesses at his trial. The reporter wrote, "He does not seem to feel as unconcerned as the other boy, and I don't think looks like a person that could commit, or assist in committing, such an act as they are charged with committing." Mann was anxious to let his father know where he was and hoped he would not be tried until his father could come to Canton. Mann added that "if he must die he will have the satisfaction of knowing that he is an innocent man."

Each boy was tried separately, with Mann's trial set for December 1 and Ohr's trial for December 8. Since there would be two trials, just one week apart, the common pleas court issued an order preventing any Stark County newspaper from publishing the testimony of the witnesses during Mann's trial until after a jury was chosen for Ohr's trial.

Mann's trial began on Monday morning as scheduled with jury selection on the first day. The court was unable to seat a full jury, so the process took half of the next day. The men selected were Hiram Hostetter, John Sommers, Obediah Williamson, Benjamin Fullon, Samuel Bleckerer, Louis Pence, George Hershey, Cyrus Zollars, David Smith, Joseph Frey, Elias Reemsnyder and Henry Weary. The prosecuting attorneys were Robert S. Shields and William A. Lynch, who had tried Amelia Richardson just three years earlier. Mann's defense team included Judson D. Lewis

Attorney Louis Schaefer assisted Robert S. Shields and William R. Day in prosecuting Gustave Ohr. Schaefer also served as a translator during the murder trial of George McMillen in 1883. *Courtesy of the McKinley Presidential Library & Museum.*

of Alliance and George E. Baldwin of Canton. Judge Seraphim Meyer presided over the case. With newspapers forbidden from publishing details of the trial, there are scant records about what happened during Mann's trial. Presumably, most of the thirty witnesses were the same for both trials. It ended on Saturday evening, and the jury deliberated only thirty-five minutes before finding Mann guilty of murder in the first degree, which is defined as murder committed deliberately with premeditated malice. In other words, he planned it ahead of time.

Ohr's trial started the following Monday morning. Again, it took a day and a half to seat a jury, which comprised C. Freedman, A.J. Hershey, R.Z. Wise, James Willis, Uriah Rhinehold, David Miller, David Sherrick, William Pence, David Lind, Joseph Beam (or Ream), Thomas P. McGinty and Ephraim Ernst. The prosecution was also led by Robert S. Shields, with William R. Day and Louis Schaefer assisting. Ohr's defense team included James M. Amerman of Alliance, J.J. Parker of Canton and T.C. Meyer. The *Stark County Democrat* reported that the opening statement Shields gave was "substantially the same statement made at the opening of the Mann trial last week." Amerman's defense argument centered on the fact that Ohr was a "young man of respectable family" and "that if a murder was committed at Alliance on June 27, as stated, Mann was the guilty party and not Ohr."

The prosecution's first witness, James Bruner, testified that he spoke to the three travelers at the railroad depot in Louisville where he worked as a telegraph operator. Wattmaugh, who was an older man, told him that his arrangement with the boys was that he would "furnish provisions for the party if they would see him on and off the trains safely," according to the December 11, 1879 edition of the *Stark County Democrat*. When the 2:00 a.m. train came, one of the boys said, "Pap, let me carry your bundle" as they headed toward the tracks.

William Westbrook, a fireman on the railroad who lived in Alliance, testified that he saw them around 5:00 a.m. near Alliance. He said he saw a coupling pin fall out of Mann's inside pocket as he was bending over to pass under a pipe. Another railroad worker named George Steur also testified that he saw Mann with a coupling pin sticking out of his coat. Next, Catharine Hunter, who owned a store near the railroad, took the stand. She said the three men had come into her store the morning of the murder. Wattmaugh bought a pound of crackers, and one of the boys said, "Pap, get some cheese." She identified the two boys the next day when she visited the jail, and she went to the undertaker to view Wattmaugh's body. They were the same three customers she had in her store the day before. Then Dr. Tressel testified that he examined Wattmaugh shortly before he died. He had wounds above each eye, on his forehead, on top of his head and on his neck that appeared to have been inflicted with a blunt object. When asked what had happened, according to Judge Meyer's summary to the jury, Wattmaugh said, "I have been murdered and robbed. We were three together—travelled together several days. The other two murdered me, and robbed me of my clothes, my money, my bundle, and all I had. I am killed for—" and he was not able to finish his sentence. He nodded when asked if two people had attacked him before falling unconscious. He did not wake up.

The jury was asked to leave the room during the testimony of John Garland, who said that he had visited the prison and heard Mann say to Ohr that even if they could prove he murdered Wattmaugh, they "could not hang him" because he was only seventeen. The jury was brought back in to hear John Gillespie, an editor and postmaster from Alliance, who also went to the prison to see the boys. He talked to Mann first. When he spoke to Ohr, he said, "[Mann] accuses you of doing the deed. He said, that is true, I am the one who did it." Gillespie said Ohr told him "they both agreed to kill the old man, but when they came to do it the other weakened."

In his summary to the jury published in the December 18, 1879 edition of the *Stark County Democrat*, Judge Meyer described the crime scene. In the area known as Webb's grove, there was a "spot of blood and traces of a streamlet of blood, where blood had flown and trickled down on the ground below, where it had formed a clot as thick as a thumb, an elevated clot. That blood was found bespattered over bricks on either side and on the ground around; that about two feet from the blood and clot of blood was found the heavy, iron, railroad coupling-pin, which Mann was seen to have concealed on his person early that morning, or one just like it, with blood spots on it, and some hair and blood at its upper and ragged end." A buckle from Mann's shoe, Mann's vest and Ohr's pants were also found near the scene.

Judge Meyer summarized Ohr's defense case as primarily a testimonial to his good character before he left the home of his mother and stepfather in Chicago. "Of course evidence of good character is always to be considered in connection with all the other facts in the case," he told the jury, "and the weight to be given to it is a matter to be determined in the sound discretion of the jury. It is, however, evident that such evidence must be less satisfactory than it would be if it extended to near the time of the homicide. In the interval, it is possible, great changes may have been effected in the character of the young man, when left to himself in his wanderings over the country, and amid new associations and influences, in want, and exposed to temptations of all kinds." The defense asked the jury to take Ohr's youth into consideration.

The jury deliberated for sixteen hours and found Ohr guilty of first-degree murder. In reporting on the verdict, the *Repository* said:

> *The testimony produced by the State was so overwhelmingly convincing that the verdict could not be otherwise. In fact if it had been possible for prosecution to have brought forward witnesses who saw the fatal blow struck, it would not have strengthened their case any, and this fact is an important feature in these unfortunate cases as it leaves no doubts in the minds of the jurors or the people at large that George Mann and Gustave Ohr are the identical boys who murdered poor old John Watsmough [sic]. As to which one of the boys was the instigator and mover in this bloody drama may never be known, or which of the two wielded the deadly coupling pin but enough is known to warrant a jury of their peers in saying that they are equally guilty in the eyes of the law, and guilty, too, of a murder, that for cold-blooded, barbarous atrocity excels anything of the kind that ever disgraced the history of this county, at least.*
>
> *An old man whose head was silvered with the frosts of many winters, guilty of no higher crime than that of administering to the wants of his executioners, is murdered in cold blood, because forsooth he had upon his person the paltry sum of $5.00 and a few little trinkets of value, and not only murdered but stripped of his clothing, and left with nothing but a garment woven with the crimson fabric of his own life's blood to cover his nakedness, permitted by an overruling providence to live just long enough to testify and the truth to tell where and by whom the bloody deed was done, and today, as one of the eloquent counsel for the State said, we are able to*

say that the blood of this murdered stranger cries from our soul not in vain for justice; and by the verdicts in these cases we proclaim to the world that in Stark County, at least, the perpetrators of such revolting crimes cannot go unpunished, and while the average citizen shudders at the thought of the closing scenes of this drama of blood and slaughter that must follow, we are compelled to say, let justice be done through the heavens.

Wattmaugh's wife and sister had traveled from Philadelphia to attend both trials. They left to return home on Monday, December 15, the day after Ohr's verdict was returned. On January 1, 1880, the *Repository* reported that motions for a new trial for each boy were denied. Mann continued to proclaim his innocence, saying that he "never struck one single blow," and maintained that if Ohr would simply tell the truth, he would be exonerated. Ohr seemed to be unaffected by the sentencing, even though he appeared to understand the severity of both his crime and its punishment. When asked if he had anything to say, he said he did not. In pronouncing the sentence, Judge Meyer said, in part, "Let me beseech you by all that is sacred, improve your time, and die not an impenitent death. Let no false hope that you will escape the doom impending over you, divert you from this all important work of preparation for eternity; your fate is sealed and certain; you will die in your young days...a dreadful example to all." After pronouncing that Mann and Ohr would be "hanged by the neck until you are dead, and may God have mercy on your poor souls," Judge Meyer burst into tears.

As Mann and Ohr awaited their trials in the fall of 1879, John Sammet of Massillon was entangled in his own crime spree, which would ultimately lead him to the gallows alongside them. On September 4, under the heading "Out of the Frying Pan, etc.," the *Repository* reported that immediately following Sammet's trial for petit larceny for stealing four ivory billiard balls, he was arrested on separate burglary charges. He was set free a week later after his grandmother Elizabeth Sibila posted his $400 bail. While the prosecution was building its case, Sammet confronted witness Christopher Spuhler on November 25, the night before the trial started, and either asked him not to testify or to lie under oath. According to the prosecution, when Spuhler refused, Sammet shot him. He was convicted on the burglary charge anyway, even without Spuhler's testimony, and sentenced to five years in prison. Sammet was indicted for first-degree murder while incarcerated.

The murder trial began on March 2, 1880. Like the trials of Mann and Ohr, it took a long time to seat a jury. The process was not completed until Tuesday afternoon, when the following men were selected: Peter Camp,

John Sammet/Sammett, a native of Massillon, was regularly in trouble with the law. He killed his acquaintance Christopher Spuhler to prevent him from testifying against him in a robbery case. *Image reprinted from* The Criminal Classes, Causes and Cures *by Daniel Right Miller (1903).*

Oliver Hawkins, Samuel Mase, Lonso Hall, Jos. Moffit, Frank Bair, Henry Snyder, Peter Numan, Jas Stutz, J.H. Conkle, Henry Bockius and Leo Sell. The prosecution was led by H.W. Harter, with Lynch and Day again assisting. The defense team was made up of Baldwin, Meyer and Piero and Amerman of Alliance and Willison of Massillon. The jury visited the scene of the murder late on Tuesday, and the trial itself would begin Wednesday morning.

The first witness was Louisa Sibila, Sammet's aunt, who testified that she heard a gunshot near her home, where Sammet sometimes stayed, on the evening of November 25 between 7:00 p.m. and 8:00 p.m. She and Sammet's grandmother Elizabeth went outside and called to him. He came in through the gate and said he had also heard a shot but didn't hear anyone cry out. The three of them went back inside and sat down in the sitting room. At one point, Sammet got up and went into what Louisa described as a "little wardrobe room." She didn't see what he did in there, and he soon came back out and read the newspaper for about forty-five minutes.

John Schworm of Massillon testified that while waiting for the train on September 4, he heard Sammet say "if he was arrested that day he would go to the penitentiary, and knew he would, and before he would go there for that he would kill that G—d d—d s—n of a b—h, Christopher Spuhler, and then they could hang him and that would be the end of it." Next, Edward Royer testified that he heard Sammet say, "G—d d—n my soul, anyway; here, I've always been a friend of the boys, and now they are squealing on me." He said he also heard Sammet say he would kill Spuhler. Next, Edward Vogt testified that on the day of the murder, he had seen Sammet at a shooting range with a revolver. He said Sammet told him, "My revolver will kill a man." Frank Grabill testified that he had seen Sammet and Spuhler together around seven o'clock the night of the murder. Philip Goble, an eighteen-year-old barber in Massillon, said he had seen Sammet and Spuhler about two weeks before the murder. They argued in front of him about what Spuhler was going to say in court.

The defense called a series of character witnesses, most of whom testified that he was "quiet and peaceable" and had a good reputation. Other witnesses said they had seen Sammet and Spuhler together often, and they had always seemed friendly toward each other. Sammet's uncle Adam Sibila testified that Spuhler had slept at their house about a week before his death. More witnesses were called who said they did not know that Sammet carried a revolver. Three witnesses suggested Spuhler could have committed suicide.

After receiving instructions from Judge Meyer, the jury went into deliberation on Saturday, March 6, 1880, at 4:00 p.m. Most bystanders expected a quick decision, but as the hours went on, many assumed there would be a hung jury. At 9:00 p.m., five hours after they were dismissed, the jury announced it had come to a decision. "When the bell rang the crowd of outsiders rushed in pell mell, and filled the court room both inside and outside the bar, almost to suffocation," according to the *Stark County Democrat*. The *Repository*'s coverage agreed: "Like mad men hundreds rushed for the court house. Streams of humanity came pouring in from all directions, and in less than three minutes one could not obtain standing room in any nook or corner of the vast court room." The *Stark County Democrat* continued, "As soon as order was secured the Sheriff brought in the prisoner, the jury filed into the box and the foreman handed the clerk the verdict." Sammet was found guilty of murder in the first degree. "The prisoner, who was apparently the most calm and collected person in the room, was returned to jail and court adjourned. Thus ended the third murder trial in this county within the past few months."

On Saturday, March 13, Judge Meyer read his sentence to Sammet before a large crowd who stood in "death-like silence." The judge noted that Sammet had led a life of crime and had tried to induce others to join him in his "marauding expeditions." He said, "Like a fallen angel, you had become a tempter, seeking to seduce your young associates into crime. Fortunately your sinister efforts proved unavailing. They showed, however, a precocity for crime on your part, formerly unknown in our county. Commencing as you did, the battle of life in a spirit of reckless lawlessness, in the natural order of things, it was to be expected that a life of crime so begun must sooner or later come to a tragical end on the scaffold. Accordingly, today it has become my duty to announce to you that inglorious but well merited doom." Judge Meyer then extolled the virtues of the deceased: "The unfortunate youth so ruthlessly and untimely slain by you, died a most noble death. He fell a victim to truth and duty. His mortal remains lie mouldering in the dust; but his memory will live, and is worthy to be perpetuated by monuments of marble and brass. By his admirable conduct in trying circumstances he found himself placed in, he left an example to the rising generation, precious, and ennobling, worthy of emulation. He died the death of a martyr." After concluding with the now familiar phrase, "and may God have mercy on your poor soul," Judge Meyer again burst into tears.

At his sentencing, Sammet remained unnaturally calm. Although Judge Meyer became choked up while reading his sentence, Sammet "stood as unconcerned as though he was simply an idle spectator, and not the poor miserable human being only waiting to hear the sentence of death pronounced upon him, and whose days on earth were numbered," according to the *Repository*. "But through it all he remained the same indifferent boy. We cannot account for such an exhibition of indifference under such trying circumstances, but can easily understand why such men can commit the crime of murder. They are simply devoid of any of the finer feelings, and we suppose, cannot help it." Sammet was escorted back to jail by the sheriff, where he joined Mann and Ohr on death row.

Two reporters for the *Repository* visited Mann and Ohr at the same time in their separate cells to interview them for an article that appeared on April 12, 1880. The boys were not allowed in the same corridor of the jail, because the authorities feared they would fight and maybe even try to kill each other, although they later reconciled and kept each other company toward the end. The article described Mann as "rather inclined to be cheerful in view of the dreadful fate that awaits him in the near future." After talking to him at length, the writer pronounced that he was guilty "only in the eyes of the law" and "his hands are not stained with the blood of the murdered one." Mann said that he had been traveling with Wattmough for more than three weeks before they met up with Ohr in Fort Wayne. The murder took place only two days later. In response to the testimony that he dropped the coupling pin hidden in his coat, he said "the witness was simply mistaken." He said it was actually Ohr who was wearing a dark coat that day. He said he was asleep when Ohr started hitting Wattmaugh, and it was the commotion that woke him up. Mann had in his possession a newspaper article and a letter from a former Sunday school teacher that both spoke to his good character. The letter characterized his childhood as difficult, due to a "cruel step mother who misused him shamefully, and drove him from home."

The other reporter found Ohr "reclining upon his couch" and reading a dime novel from the the Boys of New York series. He said that "flashy literature" was partially to blame for his downfall, and he wanted to warn boys not to read such material. "I read them until I got it into my head that I wanted to have an adventure like some of the heroes I read about," Ohr told the reporter. "So I started out on a tramp, and here I am. I didn't have to tramp, but I went just because I wanted some fun." Ohr still maintained that Mann was just as guilty as he was of the murder. "When I fell in with Mann and Wattmough, at Fort Wayne, George told me the old man had a lot of money sewed in his clothing somewhere, and that he had been trying to get it. He said he had tried to get it from him in a saloon, or when he was asleep. 'But,' said Mann, 'he wakes too easily—he's too fly, and we'll have to knock him over.' Well, we tramped along together, intending all the while to get the old man's money, until we arrived at Alliance. There George told me Daddy [Wattmough] was going to stop at Pittsburgh, where he had friends, and we'd have to do it tonight, or he'd get away from us.' So we did it the next morning. Mann says I did all the striking, but that isn't so. I began the job, and hit him with a car-link, and at that Mann went off by a tree and vomited. It made him sick. I called to him to come and help me, as the old man was reviving. George came and the old man grappled with him, and then I picked up the car-link and handed it to George and he finished the job."

Just after their arrest, Ohr had claimed that Mann was innocent. When asked about this new version of events, Ohr said his original story was not true. Ohr had intended to make it look like he had killed the old man in a fight and asked Mann to keep quiet about what had really happened, because it was the only way he could get himself out of trouble. He said that he had only cried once, when his mother came to see him and that he did not "get down on my knees and pray, or get out a bible and begin to read it whenever I hear visitors coming, like Mann does. I ain't trying to work on people's sympathies."

Sammet insisted, right up until the end, that he was innocent. On June 24, the *Repository* printed a farewell letter he wrote:

> *Canton, Ohio, 24th June, 1880*
> *Dearest Friend!*
>
> *I will write you a few lines, hoping you will promptly receive it. As this is my farewell letter. I suppose you have seen the reports and the opinion of the court. All is against me, but I bear it, with all the courage that belongs to innocence and manhood, and while my breast feels crushed and bleeding, I look to Jesus, who does all things well, and who will raise the dark could when he sees that I have borne enough. I shall put every moment on my studies, and keep cool, and hide the sorrow of an injured heart, beneath the smiling meek face. Pray for me, for I cannot explain how sad I feel in these dark hours; and how hard it is when I know I have done no wrong! but I still must keep up courage for I will have to meet a death of a murderer and on the other side I am glad I can meet a death like a martyr. I will close this letter, for the end of my life is drawing near, and this is my last farewell letter. Pray for me that you may meet me in heaven, w[h]ere we both shall live forever.*
>
> *Forget me not*
> *Your Truly Friend*
> *John L. Sammet*
> *Canton Ohio*
> *Sentence to death June 25th, 1880*
> *Farewell!*

Beneath the letter, an article titled "Jail Jettings" recorded a series of bizarre and surreal scenes inside the jail. The three boys played games together and even sang a quartet with a reporter. Ohr played the zither and Sammet played the guitar "beautifully together," and Ohr performed "touching melodies with rare skill" as a soloist. They were held in cell numbers 7, 9, and 11 on the second story of the jail.

An estimated thirty thousand people visited the jail in the two months before the hangings. On June 16, the *Repository* published an article exploring the jail itself, for those who had not ventured to see it for themselves. It described "iron floored halls" and the "awful darkness of its dungeons." The entrance to the jail was through a side door facing Fifth Street. So many visitors had been coming, the "bell for admission has been almost incessant." In the first small room past the door, one could purchase photographs of each boy, as well as poetry related to their crimes. One of the poems was likely the one Ohr had composed a few weeks after his arrest. It was printed in full, exactly as written, in the August 1, 1879 edition of the *Repository*:

> *My name it is Gustave Ohr,*
> *The same I'l never deny,*
> *Wich leaves my aged parents*
> *In sorry for to cry*
> *Its little did they ever think*
> *Wile in my youthful bloom,*
> *They brought me to America*
> *To meet my fattel doom.*
> *In bad houses of Liquor*
> *I used to take delight*
> *And consequently my associates*
> *They used me ther invite*
> *It was on that fatel day*
> *As you shall quickly see*
> *My companions they indused me*
> *To go and have a spree.*
> *It was me and that old man*
> *Laying in our money bed*
> *When I quickly jumped upon him*
> *And struck him on the head*
> *I struck him with a coupling pin*
> *Which killed him ded at heart*
> *And caused his dear and loving wife*
> *From her husband to depart.*
> *To Beloit then I quickly fled*
> *Thinking to escape*
> *But the hand of providence being against me*
> *Indeed i was too late.*
> *Then I was taking prisoner*

And brought unto my doom
To die upon the scaffold
All in my youthful bloom
My trial came on quickly
Condemned I was to die
A death upon the scaffold all
On the gallows high
My companions and associates
They all were standing near
I bid them shun night walking
Likewise whiskey and all beer.
I am thankful to the Sheriff
For his kindness to me
Likewise my noble lawyer
Who tried to set me free
And also to my clergyman
Who brought my mind to bear
I die before the public now
I solemnly do declare
The day of my execution
Twas heart rending to see
My Mother came from Chicago
To take a last farewell of me
She flew into my arms and
Most bitterly she did cry
Saying my dear beloved son
This day your doomed to die.
Now my life is ended
I from this world must part
For the murder of that old man
I'm sorry to my heart,
Let each young wild and viscious
Youth, a warning take by me
Be led by your parents and
Shun bad company.

Although Ohr and Mann were not indicted for first-degree murder by a grand jury until October, Ohr's poem indicates that he was resigned to his fate early on.

Many young women from Canton and surrounding communities visited the boys. "The prisoners sentenced to be executed have exerted such an influence on young lady visitors as to elicit from nearly all of them who have visited the jail profound pity and sometimes a surprising show of feeling on behalf of the doomed boys." The article continued, "Of course, the motive stimulating visitors have been as varied, as the color of a certain coat. Curiosity, sympathy, pity, vulgar inquisitiveness, religious interest, these and many more have incited the throng of thousands to visit the Stark county jail, a jail which will soon have a national reputation as the place of execution of three boy murderers from one scaffold."

The day before the executions, attorneys, friends and relatives of all three boys returned to Canton after an unsuccessful trip to Columbus to ask Governor Charles W. Foster to commute their sentences. Governor Foster maintained that all three had fair trials and their guilt had been clearly proven. The only argument made on their behalf was their youth, which was grossly insufficient for him to interfere with the decision of the local judge and juries. Indeed, they were old enough to commit murder, so they were old enough to die for it.

The *Repository* warned its readers that there would be large crowds of people in town, and they should be on the lookout for "pickpockets, sneak thieves, pilferers of all descriptions and intentions." The paper encouraged citizens not to leave their homes unoccupied and to lock all windows and doors, keep children off the street and safeguard any valuables. Worried about the potential for a riot, the Canton Fire Police and five militia companies would supplement the regular police force. The *Repository* also

Coming Events.

Union Dam drained, ——.
Coup's great show, June 25th.
Sewer system in Canton, 19—.
Garfield's election, November 2d.
Lake View Driving Park races, ————.
High School Commencement, June 23d.
New Lake House opening, about July 1st.
Democratic National Convention, June 22d.
Triple hanging, jail, Canton, June 25th.
Akron's Saengerfest, June 15th, 16th and 17th.
Fourth of July, two weeks from next Sunday.
Democratic County Convention, Canton, June 22d.
Stark County Democrat stops lying, millenium.
Chief of Fire Department, after the next big fire.
Go-as-you-please walking match, Canton, last of June.
Soldiers' and Sailors' Reunion, Canton, September 14th, 1880.
Soldiers' monument in Canton, —— after the soldiers are all dead.
Base Ball match—as soon as the Association is ready for business.
Temperance camp meeting, Fair Grounds, July 2d, 3d, and 4th.
Republican Congressional and Judicial Convention, Alliance, June 17th.

Although the triple hanging would take place inside the prison walls, it was a spectacle unlike anything that Canton had ever seen. Here it is listed in a column called "Coming Events," sandwiched between the Democratic National Convention and Akron's Saengerfest. *Courtesy of the* Repository.

66

cautioned that there could be conflicting feelings in the crowd: "Though to many it will be a day of sorrow, to the vulgar and heartless it may be a day of merriment. Clashing of opposing sentiment tomorrow will be of no avail, and if indulged in the motley rabble which will probably be on our streets may serve to engender serious strife."

The execution has often been described as a "public hanging," but in truth, it happened inside the prison walls and was not visible to the general public. About forty men were in attendance, including about a dozen reporters. Special equipment had to be erected in order to hang three prisoners at once. On May 6, the *Stark County Democrat* announced that Asa Mattice, of Mattice and Son in Cleveland, "has been at work, in the jail here, this week, putting up their improved triple scaffold for the execution of Ohr, Mann and Sammet." The gallows were located in the west end of the south corridor of the jail, in the shadow of the courthouse. The windows closest to the gallows were closed with iron shutters, the *Repository* described the gallows itself on June 16:

> *Three ropes with nooses are suspended from above, and hang through the opening in the scaffold through which the boys will fall. The floor of the scaffold is the width of the corridor and about 15 feet long. The doors (or fall) are about six feet long and a foot and a half wide each. When closed (or forming a part of the scaffold floor), they are supported by two iron projections, similar to a door latch, both of which can be removed by the moving of an iron bar, and this causes an instantaneous drop. At the present length of the ropes a drop of eight feet would ensue, but Sheriff Altekruse says he will shorten the ropes.*

Originally, Ohr and Mann were to be executed on May 7, but Governor Foster granted them a reprieve after Sammet's trial so that all three could be executed at once. The spectacle of a triple hanging caused many local officials to support the idea of moving executions away from county jails to the centralized location of the state prison in Columbus.

On June 25, execution day, the *Repository* printed a special second edition that was almost entirely coverage of the hanging, with biographical sketches of the murderers and their victims and summaries of the trials and sentencing of each boy. Naturally, the triple hanging stirred up memories of the execution of Christian Bachtle, which had been the last time a murderer was sentenced to death in Stark County. A long article recounted that crime.

The night before the hanging, the boys had a "good supper" that included ice cream and oranges. At around 8:30 p.m., Sammet nearly escaped, but he was caught before he could reach an exit door. Ohr was heard to say, "By God, if I would have had a revolver I'd have shot the fellow that stopped Sammet." At 9:00 p.m., Mann's grandmother came in and "had a fainting fit." The *Repository* reported, "The excitement of Sammet's attempt had not died out, the fire alarm bell rang out its dread notes, and, added to cannon booming on the square, a band playing, and the tramp and call of the military sentinels, the scene was one of rare excitement and peculiarity, and the whole gang of jail prisoners were well worked up."

Those who were allowed to witness the hanging started knocking on the prison door in the early morning hours. Sammet ordered his final breakfast of fried eggs, roast chicken and toast from the St. Cloud Hotel. He smoked some cigarettes afterward. Ohr did not want breakfast and spent some time with Reverend Kuhns and Reverend Snead. Mann did not eat breakfast either and spent his last hours in the company of Judge Meyer's daughter Clemmie, who had taken a particular interest in his case. Sheriff Henry Altekruse read each boy his death warrant separately. Ohr and Sammet were unmoved, but Mann shuddered and started to cry. Clemmie Meyer and Mann's grandmother asked Ohr, one last time, to exonerate anybody he could, but he refused, saying he had told to truth about what happened. Mann cried out, "Oh Lord I didn't do it! Oh Lord you know I didn't do it! Don't you Lord?" As Mann continued to cry, Ohr said, "I can die like a man. And I don't see why he can't."

At 10:00 a.m., Ohr wrote the following, which he asked to be printed in the *Repository*: "At the day of trial my outward appearance might have been cool and calm, but those skilled in reading faces might have seen more agony there than the pen or tongue can describe. I don't want nobody to think I'm indifferent.—G.A. Ohr." At 10:05 a.m., Miss Meyer and Mrs. Mann said their goodbyes. "The scene was a very sad one," the article said. "It seemed as if Mrs. Mann would not be able to leave the prison, but she was torn away. Miss Meyer next piteously kissed the young man as she left."

Ohr refused to eat his final meal with Mann, so he ate with the *Repository* reporter. Mann and Sammet ate together, and Sammet said, "Mann, what's the use of taking on. We ought to walk out there as if we were going to a wedding. Ain't we going to see Adam and Eve and the saints and the martyrs and the prophets? Cheer up and be a man. But look a here, Mann, either you or Ohr is telling a lie, and one of you will take the wrong road.

Which is it?" Mann proclaimed his innocence, and the *Repository* noted, "Sammet did not seem to believe him."

The boys spent their last minutes with their spiritual advisors. At 11:27 a.m., Sammet appeared on the scaffold and shouted to those he recognized in the crowd who were permitted to watch the execution. He then went back into the corridor to "make his final preparations." At 11:30 a.m., Ohr came into the corridor, "crying bitterly," but he "retained his self-possession."

Soon, their time had run out, and the three boys were led to the scaffold, each accompanied by his spiritual advisor. It was now 11:40 a.m. Ohr was first, followed by Sammet and then Mann. Each wore a white shirt with a tie, and boutonnieres were purchased for them by Ed Wikidal. Their arms and legs were tied. Ohr and Sammet called out to friends in the crowd. Mann remained silent, except to speak softly to his priest. The *Repository* recorded their final moments in great detail:

Sheriff Altekruse, assisted by Deputy Sheriff Card and Richard Powell, of Massillon, then proceeded to affix the ropes upon the condemned's necks. Ohr's was affixed first, and he looked straight into the crowd while the job was being done. The rope was next affixed to the neck of Sammet, who complained that it was too tight. Several times he asked that it be made looser, saying: "Henry, that is too tight. Can't you loosen it?"

Then the rope was put on the neck of Mann. Mann said nothing, except to repeat, "Into thy hands, Lord God, I commend my spirit." He stood gazing at his attendant, constantly moving his lips in prayer.

When all had been adjusted Sherriff Altekruse and his assistants asked the culprits if they had anything to say. The reply of each was "Nothing." The Sheriff then asked the ministers if they had anything to say; any prayers to offer, and Rev. Kuhns and Fathers Vattman and Thorpe replied, "No, let it be over."

Then the assistants and ministers bade good bye to the culprits, the latter kissing them and putting their arms around them. Then Sheriff Altekruse kissed each of the boys, and put the black caps upon them. All then stood back, and Ohr cried out, "Good-bye gentleman, Good-bye all."

Sammet repeated this, and instantly added, "God bless my poor grandmother."

Mann's last words were the prayer which he had constantly been repeating.

Sherriff Altekruse sprung the trap, and with a quick report and hushed whisperings, the three boys, at 11:43, dropped to death. Ohr moved the muscles of one leg after he was down, and that was all. Sammet did not move a muscle. Mann continued to squirm with his legs, and draw up his shoulders. Drs Conklin and Slusser were physicians for Mann, and they pronounced him dead in 8 minutes. His squirming continued for about five minutes. Drs Johnson and Schilling were the physicians for Ohr, and they pronounced his heart beating stopped in 13¾ minutes after the drop. Drs Brant and Portman were physicians for Sammet, and they pronounced his heart still in 10 minutes after drop.

At 31 minutes after the drop, Ohr was cut down. His neck was pronounced broken. Sammet was cut down ten minutes later, and his neck was broken also. Three minutes later Mann was cut down and his neck was also pronounced broken. The execution was a success, actually and professionally.

After the bodies were cut down by Deputy Sheriff Card and assistants, they were laid out upon boards in the corridor, where they will remain until night, at least. Sammet's face is a little bloodshot, but the others appear as natural as life. Thus ends the great tragedy.

Mann was buried in the English Catholic Cemetery in Canton; Sammet was buried in Massillon; and Ohr was buried in Rowland Cemetery on the east side of Canton. The triple scaffolding remained in the jail corridor for six weeks, and visitors were allowed to come view it.

4
JOSEPH KLINE

When Simon Kline, a widower and stonecutter by trade, died on the evening of December 11, 1880, in his home at the corner of Roland and Mahoning Streets in Canton, everyone assumed he had fallen victim to pneumonia or consumption, since he had been sick for at least a week. Some of his neighbors thought something was amiss, however, so they persuaded the authorities to open a case. A coroner's investigation uncovered the suspicion that he might have been murdered, and Simon's son Joseph Kline was arrested and charged in connection with his death.

Under the headline "Foul Play Suspected," the *Repository* reported that Simon's funeral had been postponed and that his son's "actions during his father's slight illness have been very strange. He is said to have reported that several physicians have been in attendance upon his father, which is known not to be true. It is reported that young Kline said in a barber shop last Thursday or Friday that he did not expect his father to live, when the patient himself said to callers that he was but slightly indisposed, the result of a cold." The article acknowledged the newspaper was printing "mainly rumors" at this time, and the paper would be glad to exonerate Joseph's name if he was found to be innocent.

In the afternoon of December 13, Coroner George B. Cock went to the Kline residence and removed Simon's heart and stomach, with Drs. Brant and Phillips. A "chemical analysis" was immediately conducted, and Joseph was arrested within hours. A coroner's inquest was held in Mayor

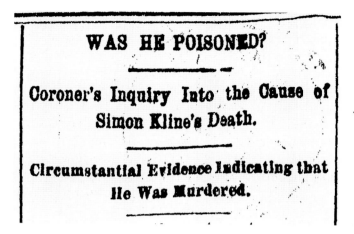

WAS HE POISONED?

Coroner's Inquiry Into the Cause of Simon Kline's Death.

Circumstantial Evidence Indicating that He Was Murdered.

Joseph Kline was almost immediately suspected of poisoning his father, Simon. This headline appeared in the *Repository* on December 14, 1880. *Courtesy of the* Repository.

James Vallely's office the next morning, and witnesses created a strong case implicating the deceased's son.

Dr. R.P. Johnson was the first witness called. He testified that Joseph had come to his office about ten days earlier and said that his father was sick but did not want a doctor to come see him. A few days later, Joseph stopped him on the street and said that his father was still sick and "if he don't get better, I'll have someone to see him." When Dr. Johnson asked what was wrong, Joseph said his father was "vomiting and manifesting a great deal of anxiety concerning his condition." Dr. Johnson said he did not prescribe any medication, although it had been reported that Joseph did in fact purchase morphine—which he said was prescribed by Dr. Johnson—at a drugstore.

Next, Lewis K. Hurford testified that he had known Simon for about four years, and he had always been in good health. He visited him during his recent illness and found Dr. D.L. Walker trying to give him medicine on a spoon, which he could not swallow. He also testified that Joseph had been kicked out of his father's home about five or six weeks earlier after the housekeeper had accused him of abusing her. On December 5, Joseph came into Hurford's store and told him his father was sick, they couldn't stop him from throwing up and they couldn't get anything to stay down.

Dr. T.H. Phillips, one of the physicians who performed the autopsy, testified that none of the vital organs examined was "in a sufficiently diseased state to cause death, but appearance indicated that death had been caused by the introduction of some poison to the system; the heart, kidneys, liver, and brain being intensely congested, and the heart was entirely free from blood, while the veins were full, and this resulted from the paralysis of the different organs by the poison introduced to the system." Dr. Phillips also testified that he had seen Joseph on the Thursday or Friday before his father's death when he came to inquire if there was a balance due on his account from his mother's illness the year before. "He seemed irritated when I told him it had not been paid," Dr. Phillips said. "He said his father was very sick and not expected to live; that he had pressed his father to send for me but he would not do it, and some of the neighbors had sent for Dr. Walker. The next morning I met Dr. Walker and inquired if Mr. Kline was very sick. He replied that he was getting well and that he had discharged him."

Dr. E.L. Walker was called next. He testified that he had not known Simon prior to being called to treat him in his late illness. He said Joseph called him, not the neighbors, and told him that Simon and the housekeeper were both very sick. He said his father had been vomiting for a week.

When I went to the house I found Mr. Kline lying upon the bed. Did not think him seriously ill. He did not think he was very sick. He complained of no pain except in his head, and ha[d] used no remedies except some home medicine. Said he had been vomiting some, and had assigned no cause for it except a cold. In my judgement the vomiting was caused by the arrest of the secretions. Visited him next on Tuesday morning and found him better. He said he felt better. The third visit was made on Wednesday morning when I found him still better. On Thursday morning I again visited him when I found him so much improved I thought it unnecessary to continue the visits. On Saturday I was called to visit him by Joseph Kline who said he was sleeping too much. When I arrived at the home I found Mr. Kline in a profound stupor. Endeavored to get him to swallow some water, but could not succeed. His breathing was slow and labored and respiration short. The pupils of the eyes were very much contracted. Don't think he could see. Bathed him in cold water, but without avail. He died by coma. Did not think there was sufficient poison to produce that death. The administration of morphine would produce that comatose condition. On Tuesday morning he asked me to give him morphine to enable him to sleep, but I refused. In his condition I think it would take three or four grains* to produce that state in a person not in the habit of taking it. Called James Thompson's attention to the contracted condition of the pupils of the eyes. Do not think of any disease that would cause that contracted condition. A person's lungs would be in a congested condition should he die from the effects of morphine.

---

* A grain is an old unit of measure: 1 grain = 64.8 milligrams. Morphine, codeine and aspirin are sometimes still ordered in grains, but most everything today is measured in metric milligrams.

The next person to testify was Martha Boyle, the housekeeper. She said she had worked for the family for seven months. She did not take care of Simon while he was sick because she was sick herself. "The day I took sick Joseph went into the kitchen to wash," she said. "I poured the water and he said he would wait on himself and told me to go into the sitting room. He was there about five minutes and then walked out to the barn. Mr. Kline came and called me, and I went into the yard. When I returned to the kitchen I took a drink of coffee from the coffee-pot and became sick immediately, my mouth, throat and stomach burning terribly. Took some pickles, apple, bread and tea, but found no relief. Think something was put in the coffee pot, but do not think it was poison. After taking the tea I began vomiting, and it continued about an hour, but the burning continued all night." She saw Simon on Wednesday, Thursday and Friday and knew he was taking medicine prescribed by Dr. Walker. She talked to Simon on Friday, and he said if the weather was nice on Saturday, he wanted to take a walk. "That was the last conversation I ever had with him," she said. She saw him Saturday morning but could not wake him up. Joseph told her he had given Simon his medicine. He never regained consciousness. She also told the inquest that Joseph had not been living in the house for two months because they could not get along. "He annoyed me around the house, and made indecent remarks and proposals and threatened to kick me out of the house." Although she never heard him make any threats toward his father, Simon had told her that he had threatened to burn the house down. On Friday morning, she saw Joseph drop a piece of paper in the stove. She retrieved it and saw that it was a label from Tonner's Drugstore. She put it back in the stove to burn.

Michael Thompson, the next witness, testified that he had known Simon for about fifteen years. He was at the house during Kline's sickness and noticed the vomiting. Thompson said Simon "seemed scared" and told him "I am afraid he has dosed me this time." He said he had been taking about a teaspoonful of Hamburg Drops.* Thompson told Simon that he was taking a pretty high dose, and he said the same to Joseph when he came into the room. He had also seen Simon improve on Wednesday and Thursday and was surprised to find him vomiting again on Friday. He said Simon told him, "Joe has given me too big a dose of medicine." Thompson said Joe was there and "seemed in a hurry to get uptown, and gave him another dose. He had scarcely swallowed it when he vomited. Joe

---

* Hamburg Drops were advertised as a blood purifier, strength restorer and cure for stomach, liver and kidney problems.

attended to him and then left." He said Simon had been extremely thirsty during his sickness.

The inquest was continued until the following morning when a Mrs. Haynam took the stand. She said she was in Simon's kitchen on Thursday morning, watching Joseph making a lot of food for his father. "That is enough to kill a well man," she said. And he replied, "What's the difference? He may as well die now as any other time. They had better be dead than lying around here." She also testified that she heard him say, "In two months I'll have a home of my own." Then Mariah Thompson told the inquest that about a year earlier, she had heard Joseph say, "My mother has not left me a dollar, but I'll burn the house down."

Then Joseph Goldsmith testified that Joseph had told him that he gave his father beef tea, which he did not want, but he "put my knee on him and forced it down." Charles Schmidt testified that Joseph had come into his barbershop on Friday and said, "I was so darn busy at the house. My father is very sick and not expected to live. I had three doctors down there and they all gave him up." He told Schmidt that his father would die that night or the next day.

H. Jarmouth, a druggist at Tonner and Company, said Joseph had come into the store on December 4 and purchased a bottle of Hamburg Drops. The next day, he came back and purchased ten grains of morphine. He said Dr. Johnson had ordered it, but he did not have a prescription. He asked Jarmouth to divide it into two equal parts. On December 9, he came in and purchased four more grains of morphine. The *Stark County Democrat*, which summarized the same coverage as the *Repository*, added, "One fourth of a grain is an ordinary dose and two grains are sufficient to kill an ordinary man." On December 12, Joseph purchased some carbolic acid from Jarmouth. Perhaps the most damning testimony came from William Geiger, who testified that on or around December 7, Joseph purchased half an ounce of arsenic from him at the Opera House Drug Store.

After all of the witnesses had spoken, Joseph was brought before the mayor to be charged with killing his father. He pleaded not guilty and was returned to jail. The following day, December 16, Coroner Cock, Prosecuting Attorney Harter and William R. Day took Simon's stomach to Edward W. Morely, professor of chemistry at Western Reserve College, in Hudson. It would be several days before the results would be known.

As Stark County waited to hear definitive proof that yet another murderer had lived among them, the *Stark County Democrat* published the following: "It is stated upon good authority that before his father's death young Kline said to several parties that he was afraid that the housekeeper would poison his father and after Mr. Kline's death he said to her, 'Well, you do all the cooking.' From this it seems that he thought the fact that his father had been poisoned might possibly become known and thought to fix the crime upon the housekeeper." Joseph had been studying law under the direction of city solicitor John C. Welty, and it appears he was anticipating which arguments could be used for and against him in court.

On Monday, January 3, 1881, Coroner Cock decided to file his verdict without the results of Professor Morely's tests on Simon's stomach contents. He determined that "Simon D. Kline came to his death by poisons and medicines administered by his son Joseph Kline," according to the *Repository*. The coroner finally received Professor Morely's report on January 7, and the *Stark County Democrat* wrote about it in the January 13 edition, noting that the entire report was not available to the public. "It was not expected that morphine would be found, although it is thought it had been administered. Morphine when taken is absorbed into the system and no traces of it are left in the stomach. Its presence is known by its action on the blood. In the case of Kline, the greatly congested condition of all the organs—lungs, liver, kidneys and so forth—indicated that the circulation had been paralyzed by some powerful narcotic. The presence of arsenic was discovered, and its corrosive action on the stomach was perceptible. From these indications, it would seem that arsenic was first employed and morphine was used to complete the last act." The article went on to say that Simon's body had been exhumed from Rowland Cemetery so his liver and kidneys could be removed and sent to Professor Morely.

Sheriff Henry Altekruse granted a reporter from the *Stark County Democrat* access to Joseph in jail—he was kept in the same cell that had housed George Mann until his execution. In the first edition of the year, the following was published:

> *Upon seeing the reporter he arose and approached the iron door with outstretched hand. He had not yet been informed of the result of the coroner's inquest, and when told what the verdict was he said: "At an inquest everything is one sided. Many of the persons who testified against me will, when under cross examination by my attorneys, say many things to my credit." When questioned about the poisoning he said: "I know nothing about it; I never did it, nor do I know if anybody else did; I do not know enough about poisoning to be able to judge whether father was poisoned or not. I have not the least doubt but that I will be acquitted after a fair*

trial." Concerning the damaging evidence of the housekeeper he said: "Part of her testimony is correct and part not. About the oxalic acid in the coffee I know nothing. She (the housekeeper) was the cause of my leaving home. Father and I were always on the best of terms. If I did buy arsenic and morphine, that is no sign that I poisoned father. I frequently used morphine, and maybe I didn't use the arsenic at all. Even if Tonner's drug clerk said that I told him that Dr. Johnson prescribed the morphine that don't settle it by any means." His arrest doesn't seem to wear on him in the least. He said: "I have plenty of good reading matter, and I manage to make the time pass pleasantly enough under the circumstances without being lonesome."

On January 27, the *Stark County Democrat* reported that a grand jury had indicted Joseph Kline for murder in the first degree. He pleaded not guilty and remained convinced that he would be exonerated at his trial, which was set for June 27, 1881.

Judge Seraphim Meyer was again the presiding judge. Prosecuting Attorney Henry W. Harter and J.J. Parker led the prosecution, and Joseph was represented by Baldwin and Shields and Anson Pease. The trial began on June 29. The state hoped to establish that Joseph's motive was a desire to inherit his father's property. They planned to prove he killed him through a series of witnesses who would provide circumstantial evidence against him and medical experts who would use the latest scientific tests to show how Simon died. The defense would rely mostly on character witnesses, calling their own medical experts to refute the state's experts, and the "alibi" that Joseph sometimes took morphine himself and had purchased arsenic to get rid of a rat problem at the home.

The state called Michael Thompson as the first witness. He was with Simon on Sunday evening, the week before his death. "The sick man was vomiting very severely and almost continuously, into a vessel at the side of his bed," Thompson said. "The vomit was of a dark greenish color. The vomiting strained the sick man very much and continued a long while. He complained of a burning sensation in his throat and stomach. He looked very pale." The following Monday, Thompson said he gave Simon roasted apples, which he threw up almost as soon as he swallowed any. Eventually, he was able to keep some down. Thompson stayed with Simon all night, and by morning, he had stopped vomiting. Over the next few days, Simon's condition greatly improved. By Thursday, he was out of bed and dressed. "The next time I saw Mr. Kline was on Saturday afternoon at about 1 o'clock. Joe came down for me, and I went to the house; found Mr. Kline lying in bed in stupor; chest heaving, sweating profusely; his eyes were shut; I was much alarmed; I remained in the room until he died, about 7:30. Joe went for Doctor Walker shortly after I arrived in afternoon; Joe said that the Doctor said he had given him nothing to cause the stupor; the doctor didn't come until Joe went the second time, as I insisted on having a doctor then." He said Simon did not move the entire time he was there. The doctor came and threw cold water on his face to try to revive him. Thompson noticed a white substance on his mouth that seemed to come from his throat and was strangling him. After Simon died, the doctor opened his eyes and his pupils were very large. On cross-examination, Thompson said he noticed two different bottles on a table near the bed that were different from the medicines he had been instructed to give Simon. He said one had a dark liquid in it. He gave both bottles and a box of quinine pills to Dr. Walker after Simon's death.

Next, John Kimes, a stonemason, testified that he stopped at Simon's house on the Thursday before his death, and while he didn't look very well, he said he was feeling much better and expected to be up and around in a few days. Simon asked Joseph to leave the room so they could discuss business, but he refused. Kimes owed Simon $14.12 for some work he had done. As he handed it to Simon, Joseph said, "Give it to me." Kimes ignored him and gave the money directly to Simon anyway.

The prosecution's star witness was Margaret Boyle, the housekeeper. She said she had known Simon for thirty-three years and had worked for him previously, but her most recent employment began on May 29, 1880, after Mrs. Kline passed away in December 1879. She had known Joseph since he was a little boy. She described what she saw the first day Simon became ill:

On Friday he made sausage. I got dinner at the usual time. Mr. Kline ate dinner and appeared well. Friday afternoon he finished the sausages. Joe came home Friday, after dinner, about 3 o'clock. His father was working at the sausage, out in the summer kitchen. Joe went out to the barn and back, came back into the summer kitchen, took down a tin cup, walked to the next neighbors and brought back water in the tin. He asked me if I would have a drink of water. I said no, thanking him. He then gave it to his father who drank of it. Joe went away shortly after. Don't think he was there over ten minutes. He did no work. Mr. Kline continued to work about an hour and a half. [He] washed and combed and went up town. He came home and into the house about dusk, with some packages, and then went out into the yard without speaking to me. He staid in the yard about 15 minutes, he had been in the privy. He came into [the] *house through the kitchen to his sleeping room. He told me then that he had been taken very sick and had cramps, that he was sick at his stomach and had a pain in his head.* [He] *said he was cramped in the bowels. He laid down on the bed lounge and threw up a great many times into a vessel I gave him. The matter vomited was yellow green. I stayed up with Mr. Kline until 10 o'clock. He had eaten no supper, because he said he couldn't. He drank water that night, appearing to be very thirsty. He remained on the lounge all evening. I went up stairs to my bedroom. Was not down again until Saturday morning at daylight. Mr. Kline was lying on the same lounge with his clothes still on.*

The next day, Joseph came over and helped her prepare dinner (the midday meal) and supper. She said he was alone in the kitchen for part of the time when the tea and coffee were being made, since she was working between the kitchen and the out kitchen at the time. Joseph gave his father some tea with his supper, and soon afterward he was "taken with a very severe attack of cramps and vomiting and was terribly sick." She said his vomit was "of an ugly slimy, green nature." She was also sick after supper that night.

Joseph slept in the same room with his father that night and already had the tea and coffee heating when Mrs. Boyle came downstairs on Sunday morning. She and Simon each drank some tea—Joseph did not—and they were both sick afterward. Joseph made dinner on Sunday afternoon, and afterward she and Simon were both sick again. "Joseph didn't seem to be affected by anything he ate," she said. Joseph made supper that evening, and again his father threw up afterward. When she got up on Monday morning, Joseph had already made breakfast. After drinking some tea, she was sick yet again. "My limbs seemed to be all drawing up. I went out to the privy, then went through Mr. Kline's room up stairs. When I passed through Mr. Kline was as bad as ever. During the rest of Monday and Tuesday I was sick in bed." She noted that Joseph did all the cooking on Monday and Tuesday.

Simon's health improved on Wednesday and Thursday, and Mrs. Boyle was also feeling much better by Thursday. Late Friday evening, Simon told her he planned to go out on Saturday. Mrs. Boyle went to bed shortly after and said Joseph "passed through my room several times during the night." When she got up Saturday morning, he said that he would not give his father any breakfast because he had given him some medicine and he might throw up. He went in a few times that morning and told her his father was sleeping. She said she would go in and clean his room, and Joseph said, "You don't need to bother." Then he asked her for the key to his father's bureau upstairs, and she gave it to him. Simon slept the rest of the morning and afternoon, and Mrs. Boyle started to grow concerned. "Joe went in the room and shook his father and tried to awaken him. I told him to awaken him by degrees because he might be under the influence of the medicine. Joe said, 'I hope father has not taken any medicine from that bottle,' adding, 'I fear father is sleeping too much.'" She said there was a rattling sound in his throat and he was sweating profusely.

Joseph sent for Michael Thompson, who was very concerned when he saw Simon. Thompson and Mrs. Boyle told Joseph to get the doctor. When he returned without a doctor, he said, "I told the doctor how he was and the doctor said he was just sleeping." They insisted he go back and bring the doctor with him. Dr. Walker came and tried to wake him up, as previously stated in Thompson's testimony, to no avail. Simon died between seven and eight o'clock that night. Joseph seemed to be rushing the funeral, insisting that it be held on Monday morning, in spite of the fact that his mother's family could not get to Canton in time from Pennsylvania. He told Mrs. Boyle he wanted his father's funeral to be on the same day as his mother's had been the previous year.

Next, Dr. Walker took the stand and provided medical details regarding Simon's condition. He said when he first came to see him, Simon was lying in bed and complaining of pain in his head. His tongue was "moist and slightly coated," his pulse was eighty and he had barely passed any urine. Dr. Walker prescribed tincture of digitalis and two grains of quinine, alternating every three hours. The next morning when he returned, Simon was feeling a little better but had still passed no urine during the night. He prescribed half a teaspoon of aslote potash dissolved in spirits of nitrous ether every three hours. He told Joseph and Mrs. Boyle to stop giving him the digitalis but to continue with the quinine. On Wednesday and Thursday, his condition was greatly improved. Dr. Walker changed the dosage of ether to three times a day and added fifteen drops of aromatic spirits of ammonia mixed with two teaspoons of port wine. Since he was doing so well, Dr. Walker discharged him. Joseph came to see him on Saturday afternoon and asked him if there was anything in the prescribed medicine that would make his father sleep. "I answered no. He said he thought his father was sleeping too much. The second time he came it was about a half hour after his first visit, and I accompanied him down to the house. I found Mr. Kline lying on his bed in the same room I had seen him before. He was in a profound stupor. He was breathing laboriously or stentoriously [*sic*], and very pallid." His pulse was slow and erratic, and he was in a cold sweat. After unsuccessfully trying to wake him, the doctor stayed with Simon until he died. Under reexamination, he added that he did not prescribe anything that Joseph would have needed to get at Tonner and Company drugstore.

Next, Coroner Cock testified that he delivered Simon's stomach to Professor Morely and later exhumed his body to retrieve the liver and kidneys. He said the ground at the cemetery was covered in snow and frozen, and the body was "well preserved." He hand-delivered the organs to Professor Morely. Next, Professor Morely, who said he had "considerable experience in poisoning matters," took the stand. He said the kidney and liver were frozen when he received them. On January 10, he used the Fresenius and Babo* method to look for arsenic, which he found. When he analyzed the contents of Simon's stomach, he found "about an ounce of brownish fluid" and an "unnatural" red patch in the stomach lining he thought could be produced by arsenic. "Arsenic is a narcotic poison and produces faintness and a sense of depression, followed by pain and sickness at the stomach, vomiting," he said. "Arsenic sometimes makes urine scanty. It is absorbed from the stomach into the blood. From the blood it is taken by the kidneys and eliminated mostly by urine. The arsenic which remains in the liver and kidneys represents only a portion of that introduced into the system. Two or three grains are generally a fatal dose."

Professor Morely also said that morphine is a poison that would produce the effects of "stupor" observed in Simon before his death. "At first you can raise the subject and he can speak," he said, "but by and by you can't raise him at all. The breathing [becomes] accelerated and stertorous. The pulse becomes low and weak. The pupils of the eyes are contracted and insensible to light. Bodily temperature is lowered and the action of the heart becomes less vigorous until the patient dies." He analyzed the medicine bottles recovered from Dr. Walker's office and said there was no trace of arsenic or morphine in either of them.

The next medical expert to testify was Dr. T.H. Phillips, who was present at the autopsy. He said that Simon's scalp and vessels covering the brain were "engorged with blood," as were the lungs and heart. "The post mortem characteristics of death by morphine is a general engorgement of

---

* In basic terms, when using the Fresenius and Babo method for determining the amount of arsenic, the scientist makes a slurry of the sample and treats it with various chemicals (in other words, acids, bases, sulfur, ammonia) to first dissolve all the metals into a solution. This eventually results in the formation of a solid containing all the arsenic extracted from the original sample. The total amount of arsenic can be calculated from the weight of the solid produced.

the vital organs with blood," he said, adding that a symptom of arsenic poisoning was "a feeling of heat in the throat and stomach." Earlier in the trial, Thompson testified that Simon had complained of a burning in his throat and stomach. Dr. Phillips also testified that arsenic poisoning would produce greenish-colored vomit, which Thompson and Mrs. Boyle also observed, in addition to a headache. When the state attorney asked him to speculate about the causes of Simon's first sickness and then his final sickness, Dr. Phillips stated that, in his opinion, the first sickness was caused by arsenic and the second by a morphine overdose. The state posed the same hypothetical question to several other medical experts, who all concurred with Dr. Phillips.

On July 5, Simon's neighbor and fellow stone contractor Daniel W. Stabler testified that on the morning of the funeral, he told Joseph that there were "strong suspicions that his father had received a dose of poison and that we wished to have the matter investigated. If he was not guilty of it he had better favor the investigation. If he was guilty he deserved to be punished. He replied, 'I will do as I please,' and walked away." It was Stabler who first alerted the authorities that Simon died under suspicious circumstances.

There were reports that Joseph had been kicked out of his father's house, and he had only returned just before his father's illness began. Mrs. Robert M. Jack testified that Joseph was boarding at her home from September until ten days before his father's death. She once heard him say that the house belonged to him, but his father had lifetime rights to live in it. Several additional witnesses testified that during Simon's illness, Joseph had told them that his father was not expected to live, in spite of the fact that the only doctor who attended to his father discharged him because he was improving. He told some of them that multiple doctors had been called to the house, when in fact only Dr. Walker had been taking care of his father.

Just as he had testified at the inquest, William Geiger told the court that he had sold half an ounce of arsenic to Joseph around December 7. He said he wanted to use it to kill some rats. Henry Jarmouth testified that he had sold Joseph ten grains of morphine, divided into two doses, which Joseph said was ordered by Dr. Johnson for his father on December 5. He asked Geiger what the dose should be, and he said between one-eighth and one-quarter of a grain. "I told him at that time that a grain would probably prove fatal," Geiger said. "I told him that an overdose might produce vomiting or sleep which could result in death. I think he asked me what the antidote was." Joseph came back on December 9 and asked for five more grains, claiming again that Dr. Johnson had sent him to get it.

After postponing the case for one day so Frank A. Perdue, a juror in ill health, could rest, the defense began presenting its case on July 8. The first witness, Dr. L. Slusser, suggested that the effects of arsenic poisoning would have happened faster than Simon appeared to get sick. The rest of his testimony largely agreed with the expert medical testimony for the prosecution. Next, Dr. Ridenour testified that the effects of arsenic poisoning could be the same as several other types of poison. He also said that someone who had been exposed to arsenic would likely be sick within a few minutes. He suggested that the cause of death could have been "brain fever or narcotic examinations." Under cross-examination, the state's attorney asked him to answer the hypothetical cause of death that had been asked of the state's medical experts. He said, "Medical science does not enable me to determine the cause of death. There is nothing inconsistent in the theory that he died by morphine."

Then the defense called Mrs. Timothy Thomas, Simon's next-door neighbor. The attorney asked her the following questions, which were objected to and sustained by the judge: "Did you know that the Kline property was infested with rats? Did you know Joe had laid poison for rats a few weeks before the death? Do you know if Joe was in the habit of taking morphine?" She was, however, allowed to answer if she had ever seen laudanum, morphine or opium in the house. She said she had not.

All that remained for the defense's case was to prove that Joseph was not the kind of person who could commit parricide. John C. Welty testified that Joseph worked in his office from December 1879 to December 1880, and Simon came in to see his son about once a week. He said they always seemed to get along well. The defense closed with a string of character witnesses, all of whom testified that Joseph was peaceable, quiet, good, "not quarrelsome" and "kind to his father and mother."

Closing arguments for both sides were given on July 12. According to the *Repository*,

> *The speakers for the defense were both rather severe on the medical expert witnesses, and the chemist, Professor Morley, insisting that the product of the chemical analysis was too meager to be taken into consideration; holding that water or tea from an old tea-pot when taken into the system, might have contained sufficient arsenic to account for the finding of the analysis. It was further insisted upon by the defense, that there was insufficient evidence to decide upon the first sickness as being caused by arsenic, and cases were cited showing that fresh pork, and other irritant poisons, had caused nearly*

similar though not so long continued attacks. As to fixing the death to morphine poisoning they claimed that neither the post mortem examination nor chemical analysis showed sufficient evidence of morphine, nor was the symptomology of the last attack of the requisite distinctiveness in the absence of positive proof that morphine had been administered, to bring in an indictment for murder by morphine administered by Joe.

In his instructions to the members of the jury, Judge Meyer explained that they did not have to be 100 percent certain but certain "beyond a reasonable doubt," which he explained: "In the trial of criminal cases absolute or mathematical certainty can never be attained, and, therefore, cannot be, and is not required. All that the law can, and does require, is that the guilt of the accused be established by that degree of certainty which is called *moral certainty*, and which is ordinarily expressed by the legal maxim that the guilt of the accused must be proven beyond the existence of a reasonable doubt." He explained that in a murder case, the evidence can be circumstantial evidence, direct evidence or a combination of both. He said, "Indeed, as most crimes are usually committed in secrecy, often in the darkness of the night, it is very seldom that direct evidence is attainable to prove the offender's guilt." He went on to say that in most cases, circumstantial evidence is the only evidence available. "Experience has shown that the criminal who has committed some secret crime such as murder, has whilst plotting and carrying out his dark deed, often left a series of traces behind him, and often become entangled in a web of circumstances, pointing with almost unerring certainty to his guilt." He explained that the state believed it had proved that Simon's death was caused by opium or morphine poisoning after a failed attempt at arsenic poisoning because he threw up so much of it. The defense believed the testimony failed to prove that it was those exact poisons that killed him, his death could have been caused by a number of other poisons and there was not sufficient proof that Joseph was the one who gave him the poison.

Judge Meyer paid particularly close attention to the reliability of scientific evidence, saying, "Testimony of learned and experienced medical experts in cases of this kind is entitled to great respect, consideration and weight… the science of chemistry has become with the advancing progress of the age, one of the most exact, and absolutely reliable of the sciences, and its results entitled to the greatest respect and consideration in the courts, criminal and civil, of our country." He also told the jury that Joseph "expected or predicted the fatal event, without apparent reason." Then they were released to deliberate at 5:40 p.m. As the jury left the courtroom, Joseph was confident he would be acquitted, and the *Stark County Democrat* reported that he even intended to sue the county for his imprisonment.

At 5:15 p.m. on Wednesday, July 13, nearly twenty-four hours after they had been released, the courthouse bell rang, indicating that the jury had arrived at a decision. The courtroom was soon filled with people. As Joseph was brought in, the coolness he displayed throughout the trial seemed to disappear, and he looked somewhat anxious. Jordan Stanley, the foreman chosen by the jury, surprised everyone present when he announced that they had found him guilty of second-degree murder, which is defined as murder "with malice but without the premeditation or previous design." The city was immediately aflutter, since it was difficult to understand how someone who was guilty of poisoning his father over several days was not guilty of premeditation. The *Repository* declared that it must be some sort of "compromise" of the jury, since the verdict "is illogical in law, and unwarranted by the evidence." The newspaper believed that Kline should have been convicted of first-degree murder, which carried with it the death penalty. Indeed, at the sentencing Judge Meyer called the decision "an inconsistent, illogical, legal monstrosity" and "utterly unjustifiable." Conviction of second-degree murder meant that Joseph would be sentenced to life in prison. The *Stark County Democrat* reported that initially the jury was split, six for conviction and six for acquittal. Apparently, Frank A. Perdue, who had been ill during the trial, wanted the jury to agree on a verdict so he could go home. The newspaper suggested his health was a contributing factor to the compromise verdict.

On the morning after the verdict, a reporter with the *Repository* visited Joseph in jail. He was dressed neatly and smoked a pipe. The article noted that he was now in the cell in which Gustave Ohr had been confined the previous year. He told the reporter that he didn't think he had a fair trial. "I would have proved my innocence if my best testimony had not been ruled out," he said. "I am anxious to hear that the motion for a new trial has been filed, and if it not granted my case will be carried up to the Supreme Court. If I must go to the penitentiary, I will go with the full knowledge that I am a martyr to the errors of my trial, but will have the comfort of knowing that I am innocent."

Joseph did not get another trial. On July 15, Judge Meyer sentenced him to life in prison, "and there kept at hard labor," except when in solitary confinement for the first five years, and then solitary confinement for the first six months of each year for the remainder of his life. Further, the judge ordered him to pay for the costs of his trial. It was reported years later that physicians at the prison refused to follow the order for solitary confinement.

On July 19, the *Repository* published the following curiously worded notice under a column of news from Massillon: "Joseph Kline, formerly of Canton, but who will hereafter be a resident of Columbus, paid Massillon a short visit last night, and stopped at Marshal Paul's Hotel. At 5 o'clock this morning he proceeded to Columbus in company of Sherriff Altekruse." It was later learned that officials chose to leave from the Massillon train station, rather than Canton, to avoid the crowds. A few days later, the *Stark County Democrat* republished a report from Youngstown that appeared in the *Cleveland Herald* on July 15: "Youngstown readers have taken a deep interest in the trial of Joseph A. Kline of Canton. He resided here for some time and married Miss Eliza Petri, daughter of Mike Petri, a wealthy citizen of this place. Mr. and Mrs. Kline lived here awhile, but the husband was so lazy that the father-in-law had to ship them. They went to live at Canton, where he ill treated her and refused to provide the necessaries of life. Mr. Petri brought his daughter home a year or two ago. She has since secured a divorce, and has married a man named Graber, porter at the Tod House."

This would not be the last time Stark County heard from Joseph Kline. He next appears in the historical record on July 10, 1890, when he sent a letter about prison life on the Fourth of July to be published in the *Stark County Democrat*. After breakfast at 7:30 a.m., exercise from 9:00 a.m. to 10:30 a.m. and some patriotic songs and readings,

> *The prisoners were then marched out and given the freedom of the lawn, until dinner time, to engage in such sports as they saw fit. The prison was beautifully decorated with bunting and flags. Much credit is due to the daughters of our worthy warden and deputy, for the display of taste in the decorations. The bill of fare for dinner was new peas, new potatoes, nice light bread, pound cake, and pie, with lemonade to wash it down. At 2 o'clock the prisoners were again allowed the freedom of the lawn to enjoy themselves until 6 o'clock. And as we once more resume the daily prison rank, we will look back to the Fourth of July as a bright oasis in the Sahara desert of our prison life, and our prayer to God is that his choicest blessings may rest upon our kind warden, and all his assistants.*

> *From an old Canton boy,*
> *Joseph A. Kline*

The following year, on January 15, he again wrote to the *Stark County Democrat*, this time imploring Stark County's citizens to work on his behalf for his release. "I have now served over nine years for a crime of which I am innocent," he said. "I protest to you in the name of the great and loving God, the Father of us all, and who searches and knows all the secret thoughts and desires of our hearts, that I am innocent of the crime of which I am charged with." He wanted people to write to Governor James E. Campbell on his behalf to get him a pardon. On August 29, 1895, the *Stark County Democrat* reported that Joseph's friends had organized and were petitioning Governor William McKinley for his pardon. The article noted that he had been selected as the warden's runner, from a total of 2,200 prisoners, and he had been a "model prisoner" for the past fourteen years.

After Joseph Kline served nineteen years in prison, Governor Asa S. Bushnell finally granted him a Thanksgiving pardon in 1899, based largely on his spotless prison record. When it was announced by the warden in the chapel during the Thanksgiving service, "Tears came to the eyes of others who had hoped the pardon would come to them, but all applauded. Kline sat in silence."

When he was released, Joseph came to Canton to visit the graves of his parents but chose to live with a relative in Pennsylvania instead. "I do not wish to remain in this city, the scene of my sadness," he told the *Stark County Democrat*. The article noted that he had "changed considerably in appearance since his incarceration and his friends were hardly able to recognize him." A separate article in the same edition noted that prisoners had great respect for the court system in Stark County, and criminal cases tried locally were "the subject of much discussion" by the prisoners. After his release, Daniel Stabler, the man who had first suspected Joseph and was now an elderly man, told the *Stark County Democrat* that he was "sorry to hear that he was released but as long as he don't call around here it will be all right. I don't think he should have been given his freedom." Joseph stayed out of trouble for the remainder of his life and disappeared from the historical record.

5

GEORGE McMILLEN

Less than a year after Joseph Kline was convicted of killing his father, another terrible murder once again shocked the community. In the early morning hours of June 15, 1882, George McMillen shot his wife, Augustine, in her bed "in the dead of night," inside their house on South Cherry Street in Canton, near the east bank of Nimishillen Creek. The first article about the crime in the *Stark County Democrat* began with astonishment before reporting on the actual crime: "The supply of murder cases in Stark County appears to grow no less with the lapse of time, and every term of the criminal court does not appear to be complete unless there appears on the docket one or more cases of homicide, and no sooner does one disappear than another is ready to take its place in the category."

The article continued to report on the latest murder. Officer Thomas Baughman heard a gunshot at 2:05 a.m. while on duty at the corner of Charles and Cherry Streets. Soon afterward, he heard screaming. "He immediately blew his whistle for assistance and then started down until he came to the house of George McMillen," the *Stark County Democrat* said. Officer Baughman found George in his neighbor's backyard, yelling that he had been shot. Officer Bechtel arrived on the scene, and the two policemen went upstairs, "into a poverty stricken appearing attic, containing two beds, and in the one at the north end the woman, Mrs. McMillen, was found weltering in her blood, flowing from a pistol shot wound in the region of the left eye, from which the life current, commingled with brains, exuded in a sickening stream." She died twenty minutes later.

GEORGE M'MILLEN.   **AUGUSTINE M'MILLEN.**

As part of the coverage of his execution, these images of George and Augustine McMillen appeared in the *Repository* on July 20, 1883. *Courtesy of the* Repository.

George's wound was on his right breast, just over his fourth rib, and officers on the scene suspected it was a self-inflicted wound after he shot his wife. There were burn marks on his clothes, indicating that he had been shot at close range. The *Stark County Democrat* noted, "His wife did not bear a good reputation and visits of outsiders were frequent in her locality, and the murder probably grew out of the 'waywardness of women' and the improvident nature of the husband, who followed no legitimate line of honest industry, and as the police state was simply 'a curbstone ornament.'" George and his father, James McMillen, who was in the home at the time of the murder, were both arrested at 7:00 a.m. The murder weapon was not found at the scene, and police believed George had thrown it into the marshy wetlands nearby. Officer G.A. Wielandt later testified that he searched the home and the surrounding area thoroughly, and one could "stick a pole in the muck in the bottom of the run in some places, eight or ten feet." No weapon was ever recovered.

The rundown house was described unfavorably in the *Stark County Democrat*: "The house is a little story and a half affair, boarded up and down and unpainted, standing at the foot of Cherry Street, next to the creek, with two rooms down stairs, the front one carpeted and rough plastered, and the kitchen unfinished; upstairs is an attic with bare floor and two beds, and couple of 'shake downs,' that evidenced sleeping accommodations when the bedsteads were occupied. The whole place betokens the most abject poverty."

From the beginning, George claimed that a woman, whom he later identified as Fan Killin, had shot him and his wife. A week after the murder, the *Stark County Democrat* reported, "Nothing definite is yet learned as to who shot Mrs. McMillen, and all clues and traces are singularly absent." Nevertheless, George was charged with the murder, to which he pleaded not guilty. His story, as printed in the *Repository*, was a very different version of events that night:

> *During the night, he could not say at just what time, he was awakened by a noise, and upon partly arising from bed, discovered a woman in front of him, who immediately fired one shot at him and then started for the stairs leading to the kitchen. The shot stunned him, but he followed her down the stairs where she was lost from sight. The rear door being opened he stepped out and called for help, and hearing the policeman's whistle called for police, and then returned to the house and aroused his father. He then went over to the next neighbor's, Mr. Robson, a distance of about thirty feet, and asked to be let in, that he was shot. Robson and his wife were aroused, but did not open the door. As he was about to go back to his house Officer Baughman met him.*

George said he did not know who the shooter was, and he claimed that he did not know his wife had been shot. His father seemed to corroborate his story, saying he was awakened by the second shot and heard George yelling from upstairs to go to his mother-in-law's house. He claimed he was "scared and confused," and "just as he went out of the front door a woman whom he thought was George ran down stairs and out back through the kitchen."

Several family members who lived in the neighborhood gathered at the scene and immediately accused George of killing his wife and shooting himself to make it look like someone else had done it. He did not deny that they often argued, but he said he "loved her too well to kill her." Her mother, Margaret Bourquin, told the *Repository* that her daughter had recently admitted she was afraid of her husband. Augustine's family told authorities he had threatened to kill her before and had actually been arrested for trying to poison her when they lived in Carroll County seven years earlier. While the preliminary hearing was going on, the *Stark County Democrat* republished an account from the *Carroll County Chronicle* that included some backstory about the couple. George had been a coal miner. Other accounts reported that his character was questionable from an early age, when he was considered smart, but bad. He kept company that was "fast" and was described as "careless and shiftless" with "reckless habits." When the couple left Carroll County, they said they were heading to Michigan but apparently settled in Canton instead. The McMillen family was considered "quiet and inoffensive," but George and Augustine had a reputation as a "bad set." George had been acquitted of attempted murder before, which many thought was "strange," given the evidence against him. A doctor had testified that he sold strychnine to George ten days before the poisoning, and another doctor testified that Augustine had definitely been poisoned by strychnine. George admitted buying the poison, but like Joseph Kline, he claimed he bought it to kill rats.

In October, a grand jury indicted George for first-degree murder. His trial was set for December 11 but later postponed until February 19, 1883. As seen in previous murder cases, it was difficult and time-consuming to impanel a jury. The following men served: W.A. Robertson, W.H. Shipe, Robert Reinoehl, Daniel Levers, Israel Metz, C.J. Zigler, Wm. Raynolds, Frank Gaskill, George Shearer, T.B. Nerohon, George Kingsberry and Peter Lawrence. Prosecutor Henry A. Harter was assisted by J.J. Parker, and George E. Baldwin and Robert S. Shields made up the defense's legal team, earning high praise from the *Stark County Democrat* for their efforts to free their client. The judge was Anson Pease, who had succeeded Judge Seraphim Meyer as judge of the court of common pleas in February 1882. The large courtroom was packed with spectators every day of the ten-day trial.

The state opened its case with medical experts. Dr. Phillips testified that a postmortem examination of Augustine, while she was still lying in her bed, found no other injuries on her body except the gunshot wound just above her left eye, indicating there was not a struggle. Powder marks on her skin indicated she had been shot at close range. He and Dr. Johnson removed her scalp and the upper part of her skull and found the bullet lodged in the lower hemisphere of her brain. Dr. Phillips also examined George's wound that night. He said the bullet had entered his body at an angle that suggested the gun was fired upward, the bullet passing through his right breast and up into his armpit and striking no bones. His shirt was burned around the hole, indicating he was also shot at close range. The doctor said the wound could have been produced by a person "firing at himself with the left hand." Dr. Cock, who was still coroner at the time of the murder, thought Augustine had been shot within three inches, "perhaps right against the head."

Louis Schaefer was called in as an interpreter, because Augustine's mother, Margaret Bourquin, did not understand English well. She testified that she lived nearby and saw her daughter, whom she called "Gust," every day. A week before the murder, Bourquin said she went to their house and George was writing a letter to his father asking him to take him and his wife to Congress Lake. Augustine said, "I don't want to go to your folks, they abuse me too much. I like better to stay all alone with mother, and tend to her and have her tend to me." Bourquin said George had replied, "If you don't come with me I'll send a nail in your head before you go." She said that George had threatened Augustine in front of her as recently as three months before she was murdered, saying, "If she don't do as I want her to I will kill her." She said she never heard him accuse Augustine of adultery.

Next, Andrew Ramie testified that he had seen George and Augustine at a dance at Klopfensteines' Hall not long before the murder. Ramie heard him say, "That g—d— bitch ought to be killed" to a group of men down in the bar room. Back in the dance hall, he heard George ask his wife to go home. "She said she was engaged to dance with Mr. Cunningham next set," Ramie said. "[She] said, 'as soon as I dance with him I will go home.' He said, 'You d— bitch, you are never ready to go home." Then he left.

Next, Henry Culby, a carpenter who had done some work on the McMillen home around the time of the murder, testified that he "saw difficulty between them often." He said he had heard them both use very bad language while arguing about bricks for a flue and a coal bucket. Culby saw George drive over the coal bucket, which Augustine's mother had given her, and she said, "You d—d s— of a b— you can't buy me one, but you can break one given to me." He said, "I'd just as leave drive over you and break your damned neck." Later, Culby heard him say, "Such d—d women ought to have their throats cut." Augustine heard him and said it would be "better if they were both out of the world." Culby added that George had asked him to buy a pistol, but he refused to help him get one. A neighbor, David Merriman, testified that his home was about eight feet from the McMillens', and he often heard them fighting. He said he heard him "make a threat against his wife. He ran after her around the house and swore he would kill her if he could catch her."

Augustine's brother, Frank Purney, testified that he had heard George accuse his sister of adultery. He said about a year before the murder, George had a six-shooter .22-caliber revolver. He said he told his sister she should not let a woman named Fan Killin stay at their house overnight because she had a bad reputation. He told both of them that they should try to "live quietly together," about six or seven weeks prior to the murder. John White, a coal miner, said he saw George about a month before the murder at the fairgrounds. George said he and his wife were not getting along. "He bought a revolver of me then," said White. "I gave it to him in a horse stall, no one was present. [It] was a small 7-shot cartridge revolver." Officer Baughman then testified that after he was in jail, George said he had not owned a revolver for over year.

The defense began presenting its case on February 26, calling George's father, James McMillen, as the first witness. He said he arrived in town before dinner on the day of the murder, but George and Augustine were not home. He went to Margaret Bourquin's house and got the children, who were with her, and put the three younger ones—Frankie, Robbie and August (some accounts list the third son as "Willie")—to bed. The oldest girl, Jennie, spent the night with her grandmother. He saw his son and daughter-in-law when they got home, around 11:00 p.m. He helped put their horses away. "During this time they talked together and appeared glad because I had come," he said. "[They] talked over what they would do the next day." He said he slept downstairs in the front room and went to bed first, leaving them in the kitchen. They went to bed soon after. The next thing he knew, George was shouting that he had been shot. James got up to go get help, but it was so dark he couldn't find the door. He said he heard only one shot, and it sounded like it came from the street. He continued, "[I] heard someone running down stairs as I thought. I opened my door when George came down the stairs. [I] saw him near the stove. He went out the kitchen door and I followed him out. The outside kitchen door was wide open. I went over to her mother's and told her that George was shot." He said George told him and the police that Fan Killin had shot him.

Several neighbors testified that they had gone past the McMillen home on the night of the murder and saw a man and a woman sitting on the front step. Then a number of character witnesses testified that they had never seen the couple argue and George always treated his wife well in their presence.

The next day, eleven-year-old Jennie took the stand. She said that when she came home from her grandmother's house on the day of the murder, Fan Killin and Tom Renick were outside and wanted to see her mother. Later, at the scene of the murder, she remembered that the police had asked her father who shot him. "He said he did not know," Jennie said. "I said it must have been that bad lady that was there the same night." She said that Fan had recently asked her if the creek near their house was deep enough to drown someone. She also said she never heard her father say anything threatening to her mother.

The defense then started building a case that Augustine was the one who had been abusive, not George, and she was often out gallivanting, leaving him at home with the children. Susan Bombeck, another neighbor, said about three years before the murder she heard Augustine say to her husband that she would "take the heart out of him and make him eat it." Emma McCauley testified that Augustine often stayed out until late at night and George didn't complain about it. "She would tell him that he was a d— liar and called him a d—l—s— of a b—," she said. "He never used any violence against her." She said she also heard Augustine say she would "knock his brains out with a hatchet" and George "went out and cried." Another neighbor, William Murphy, recalled that he once heard Augustine call him all kinds of names, but George did not respond.

The defense rested their case on February 28, and the prosecution called new witnesses to discredit George's father James, including several coal miners who worked with him. William Skinner, a police officer from Salineville, where James lived, said, "His general character is not good. I would not believe him as readily as other men, on oath." Salineville Mayor Ferrell said "His reputation for truth has been questioned." Dr. Phillips was recalled and said that on the night of the murder, James had told him that he first saw George coming in the back kitchen door, not coming down the stairs as he had testified. Robert Killin, Fan's father, provided her with an alibi, saying she was at home with him at the time of the murder.

By the end of the trial, it was clear to everyone, including the defendant, that there would be a murder conviction. "Even the prisoner felt so," wrote the *Stark County Democrat*, "for his face was pinched and pale, and as the Judge remarked to the reporter today, 'He has looked like a dead man for the past week and knew he was lost.'" The jury began deliberating at 12:30 p.m. on Friday March 2. When the courthouse bell rang at 1:45 p.m., everyone thought the jury had reached a decision. "The streets were black with people," the *Stark County Democrat* said, "old and young, male and female, all running as fast as possible to get in, jamming on the stair cases, falling and trampling over each other, and in five minutes the large room was filled to its utmost capacity, only to find that the [bell] was sounded for opening the afternoon session of court." By 6:15 p.m. the jury was ready to announce their decision: George McMillen was guilty of murder in the first degree. The *Stark County Democrat* noted, "The statute prescribes 100 days between sentence and day of execution, so the wife murderer has yet remaining a little over three months of life."

George remained calm in the courtroom but reportedly "broke down completely" when he was returned to his cell.

On March 8, Shields made a motion for a new trial, which was denied. Judge Pease then asked the defendant to stand, saying:

> *Mr. McMillen you have been convicted of the highest crime known under the law; you have had a fair and impartial trial and have been ably defended by counsel, who have left nothing undone which would be of any benefit to you. The jury was selected with great care and they are all good, impartial men, who carefully weighed and deliberated over the testimony as brought forth, and I can say that in view of the same, I do not see how they could have arrived at any other verdict than the one they have brought in, and it now becomes my painful duty as an officer of the law, to pass sentence upon you. The statute provides that any person convicted of the crime of murder in the first degree shall forfeit his life, and I now ask you if you have anything to say why sentence of death should not be passed upon you?*

George responded, "Nothing more than that I am innocent; I am not guilty of the charge." Then Judge Pease sentenced him to hang on June 22. The article concluded, "It is somewhat singular that he should offer to plead guilty of murder in the second degree sometime ago and on sentence day claim that he is innocent. These two facts are hard to reconcile."

Three weeks before the execution, the *Repository* wrote that George was not doing very well in confinement. He told a reporter that he had not eaten anything in several days. "He was lying on his bed and hardly able to converse," the article said, "his jaws being very sore and he complained of considerable pain. He attributes it to a fall he had last Sunday while in the corridor. All the nourishment he has had has been milk." He continued to maintain his innocence and denied that he ever agreed to offer a guilty plea to second-degree murder. He viewed a lifetime behind bars as a punishment equal to execution.

One week before the execution, George asked a reporter from the *Repository* to come visit him, claiming he had a "secret" to share. As the two men talked, the prison was full of the sounds of the carpenters who were building the scaffolding for his hanging. George told the reporter that in January 1882, his wife had come and sat on his lap and said, "I have something to tell you, but will you promise not to tell it?" She proceeded to tell him that the previous Friday night, Fan Killin had come to their home with a man named Murphy, who was a detective in

Cleveland, and asked to spend the night. At one point, Murphy left to get some liquor at a nearby saloon, and Fan told Augustine that he had some money and she intended to drug him so she could steal it. Ultimately, George claimed, the man died, and Fan and his wife carried him out to the barn and covered him with straw. He said he went out to the barn and saw the man, whose "neck was being partly eaten by rats." While they were out there, Fan came by and was very upset that Augustine had "given the affair away." George left at that point and said he did not know who took the body away, but it was gone when he returned. He said his wife was worried that something was going to happen to them. When asked why he had not produced this information sooner, during his trial, he said that he "loved his wife and desired to conceal her share in the crime. But now that his days on earth are numbered, and are very few, he desires to meet his God with a clear conscience." No one in the Cleveland Police Department could recall a detective named Murphy, and it seems unlikely that George, facing the death penalty, would have withheld this vital information during his trial. Nonetheless, Canton was aflutter with this new information.

Four days before the execution, the *Repository* described the scaffolding in great detail:

> *The machine consists of a platform supported upon the scaffolding, and occupying a space of but 4x5 feet when in operation, a box two feet and six inches by four feet being required to transport it when folded. On the platform are two trap-doors opening, of course, downward. These are kept in place by two steel bolts, immediately under the joining seam, of such strength as to sustain a weight of 600 pounds. Between the double door, of which the platform is composed, these steel bolts are connected with levers on each side, which are in turn connected by a series of compound levers in the rear of the trap, the combination being concealed, but the handle of the lever extending three feet above the floor, in order that it may be easily grasped by the operator.*

The article noted it was constructed by Colonel Asa Mattice, and it was the same trap used for the triple hanging of Gustave Ohr, George Mann and John Sammet two years earlier. The article also mentioned that it could be "erected or taken apart in fifteen minutes."

Two days before the execution, George spun yet another tale for a *Repository* reporter about what had happened the night his wife was killed.

This time, he claimed that when he heard a noise and sat up in bed, there was not just a woman in his room, but a man was with her too. After she shot him, he heard the man say, "What made you shoot George?" and immediately he recognized his father's voice. The woman, who he still claimed was Fan, and his father then ran downstairs, and he ran after them. He claimed that his father was "somewhat under the influence of liquor" that night and that he had never liked his wife and had often "asserted she ought to have been killed before." It was a fanciful story that didn't make much sense, but it was printed in full anyway, likely to sell more newspapers.

The night before the execution, J.J. Parker, who had assisted with his prosecution, dropped by the jail to see how George was doing. George maintained that he had now spoken the entire truth about what had happened, and Parker told him that his stories were "mere creatures of his imagination." Parker said, in the presence of the reporter, that he had suspected that father and son "conspired together to do the crime" but that George had actually killed Augustine, and after they went outside, his father "carefully pressed George's shirt against his body so that he could wound him without danger of shooting too deep." The *Repository* article goes on to say, "This highly interesting statement of the assisting prosecutor may not have been intended for publication, but it is intelligence which the public has a right to have." George was quite talkative and chattered away with the reporter for most of the night. He did not sleep at all. Three hours before McMillen's scheduled execution, Robert Shields arrived at the courthouse, fresh from the early morning train from Columbus, with a thirty-day reprieve from Governor Charles Foster. George's execution was postponed until July 20. "And so the grim and hungry gallows within three hours of enjoying its meal of humanity, is cheated again," wrote the *Repository*. George's implication that others were involved in the murder was generally considered the reason for the reprieve.

George's father arrived at the jail that morning, expecting to attend his son's hanging. He had not yet heard about the reprieve or George's latest "confession" implicating him in the murder of his daughter-in-law. In response, James repeated the exact same story he had told in the courtroom. The only detail that was slightly different was that he was not as confident that he had heard someone go down the stairs before George came down. The house was not well built, and the *Repository* writer suggested that James might have mistaken the creaking of the upstairs floorboards as George got out of bed for someone coming down the stairs.

James wanted to publicly refute the accusation, so he requested a notary and a stenographer, and he marched into George's cell and sat down. The following was recorded:

"Well, George, I want to ask you why you are trying to fetch me into this."

"I come to the conclusion that I have to do it, as I might as well do it at one time as another."

"But what cause have you for it?"

"I think you ought to know. You know well enough that you and Fan Killin were there that night, and you asked her 'Why did you shoot George?'"

"I would have to say that I didn't say a word like that."

"Do you remember the night then that old man Silvers was there and come to our house? Didn't you see Fan Killin that night?"

"No, I never saw Fan Killin in all my life. I know I didn't."

"You didn't see her that night of the killing, did you?"

"Indeed I did not."

"What answer did you give me in the Mayor's office when I asked you if you didn't have Guss' cloak on when you were up in the room with Fan Killin?"

"You didn't say that Fan Killin was there. Not a word of it at all. Why, George, what makes you talk like that? You know that it is not true, not a bit of it. I have always been a father to you, and you shouldn't try to fetch me into it."

"It is the truth, and you know it. You don't want me to go to the scaffold with a lie on my lips? I kept it back as long as I could, and I thank God I can go now with no lie in my heart."

"Why didn't you tell this on the trial?"

"I tried to keep it as long as I could."

"Why didn't you tell him [Frazer of the Repository, pointing to him] *of it on the morning of the shooting?"*

"I tried to keep it as long as I could….When I first hallowed, where was you? Didn't you run down stairs first?"

"When I answered you, wasn't I down stairs?"

"Yes. You answered me as soon as you got downstairs."

"Go your length, George. Go your length. If I could only see why you are taking this turn against me. Because you must suffer, do you want others to suffer the same way for nothing?"

The conversation continued, back and forth, the father denying each wild accusation pitched forth by his son. James also said he only had two beers that day—one in Louisville and one at George's house. He was not drunk. The exchange took up two and a half full columns in the June 22 edition of the *Repository*. Apparently, this deathbed confession was enough to sway public opinion; the next day, the *Repository* wrote, "The public are divided in their views of the murder, but nearly every one seems to believe that James McMillen, the father, knows more than he has related about the tragedy."

In spite of all the hoopla he created at the eleventh hour, George was not given a new trial—nor was his sentence commuted to life in prison. The night before his hanging, George did not sleep. He stayed up talking, writing and smoking. During the night, he apparently could not resist telling one more tall tale, claiming that a woman had brought him a small vial of arsenic after his reprieve so that he might kill himself instead of facing life in prison if his sentence was commuted. He failed to produce said vial and later claimed he had thrown it down the privy hole in his cell. He also said he planned to slit his wrists with broken glass or a knife, both of which he claimed to have "concealed" in his cell, and bleed to death before he could be executed.

In the morning, he was served his last meal: eggs, mutton chops and coffee from the Model Coffee House. The Beach City Guards arrived just before 8:00 a.m. and took their places at the entrances of the prison and in the jail yard. At 9:20 a.m., Reverend Osbourne entered his cell, which the *Repository* noted was the same cell where the priests had given George Mann his last sacrament three years earlier. The two men prayed together. He expressed a desire to see his children and started to cry. He begged someone to bring his children to him, and he lamented their future—especially his daughter. "Boys can take care of themselves," he said, "but girls need looking after. See that she is kept out of bad company. Let her join what church she wants to, but let her keep off the streets." At 10:00 a.m., his mother-in-law came with the children, which the *Repository* described as "the most agonizing scenes ever seen within the walls." The children stayed twenty minutes, and as they were led away, George cried out, "Good-bye, good-bye, for ever." He spent his final minutes in his cell sobbing.

At 11:07 a.m., Sherriff Altekruse, Andy Danglizer and Levi McKinney led George to the gallows. The sheriff asked if he had any last words. "All I have to say is I am innocent," he said from the scaffold. "I die for my father and a prostitute. I am an innocent man. That's all I have to say." He complained that the rope was too tight around his neck. A few minutes later, the sheriff "sprung the trap, and the body of George McMillen dropped with a thud to the death to which stern justice had sent him. The drop fell at 11:12, and in seventeen minutes he was cut down, life pronounced extinct." His body was taken to Salineville for burial.

George was right to worry about his orphaned children. After his death, both sets of grandparents wanted custody. In the end, they stayed with Augustine's mother, Margaret Bouquin, in Canton. Jennie found herself entangled with the law several times, including charges of assault and indecent exposure when she was still a teenager. She tried to commit suicide in June 1889 by ingesting rat poison. In 1891, she was arrested for stealing fifty dollars from a man named Stephen Spangler, who was heavily intoxicated at the time. In 1895, she was arrested for trying to burn down a house, and in 1897, she was arrested for "removing mortgaged property." After that, she disappears from the historical record. In 1891, Robert McMillen was arrested for "being a disorderly juvenile." According to the *Repository*, he was sentenced to the "reform farm," where his younger brother August had been sent earlier that year. It was August's second stint at the Lancaster Industrial School; he was sent there the first time for theft and the second time for truancy. In 1894, Robert pleaded guilty to assault and battery and was sentenced to the workhouse to pay off a one-dollar fine and his court costs. In 1897, he was arrested for stealing a set of horse harnesses. In 1910, he and his wife, May, were arrested for assaulting a man with a brick. Robert filed for divorce later that year, claiming that May smoked cigarettes, drank intoxicating liquor, neglected her household duties and committed adultery. He asked for custody of their seven-year-old daughter, Orpha, and alimony. Frank McMillen does not appear in any Canton newspapers. He either left town or was the only McMillen child who did not lead a troubled life. Their mother, Augustine Purney McMillen, was buried with her family at Rowland Cemetery. George's father and Fan Killin were never tried for her murder.

6

HENRY POPP

n the late afternoon of April 2, 1890, after being thrown out of a saloon on East Tuscarawas Street repeatedly for drunken behavior, Henry Popp, thirty-one, returned with his pocketknife at the ready and slit the throat of owner Mortiz Grether. Within an hour of his arrest, an extra issue of the *Repository* was on the press with details about the murder. The next morning, a reporter was permitted to interview Popp, and he said:

> *I am sorry for what I have done, but Grether treated me very bad. I only learned of his death at a late hour last evening and it makes me feel very bad, although when the deed was committed I was too drunk to know what I was doing, and I blame my companions for not taking me away from that place when they saw how enraged I was. Since learning of Grether's death I have been unable to sleep or eat, it so upsets me. Last night I ate a hearty supper, but since then I hardly know what has happened. I think that I am going crazy, for my head aches so.*

Officials at the jail told the newspaper that Popp had spent most of the night crying, periodically shouting, "I am so sorry." Anything that Popp could use to commit suicide, including bedsheets and suspenders, were removed from his cell after a fellow prisoner reported that Popp said he intended to take his own life at the first opportunity.

On the night of his arrest, Popp told Sheriff Krider that he had wanted to hear the band play at Grether's saloon, but after being thrown out several

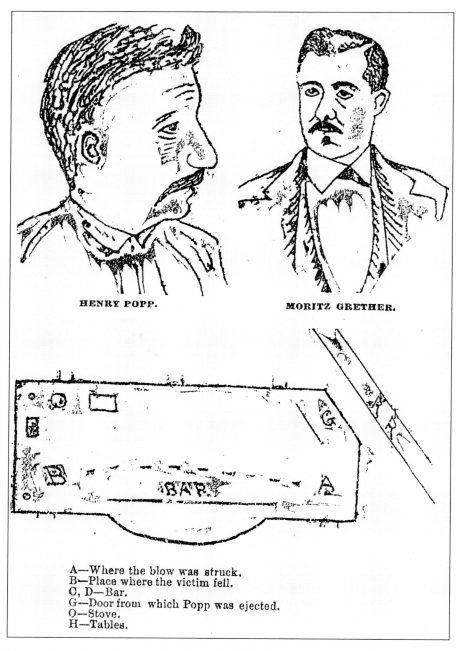

HENRY POPP.

MORITZ GRETHER.

A—Where the blow was struck.
B—Place where the victim fell.
C, D—Bar.
G—Door from which Popp was ejected.
O—Stove.
H—Tables.

Henry Popp and Grether with drawing of bar. The day after Henry Popp killed saloon owner Mortiz Grether, this image appeared in the *Repository* on April 3, 1890. *Courtesy of the* Repository.

MURDER MOST FOUL!

An Atrocious Homicide in Drunken Frenzy!

A Prominent German Saloon Keeper Fatally Stabbed!

Moritz Grether Bleeds to Death--Henry Popp, His Murderer, Commits the Fiendish Deed with a Pocket Knife.

Headline "Murder Most Foul." The *Stark County Democrat*, which was a weekly newspaper, printed this headline about the Henry Popp murder in the April 10, 1890 edition.

times, he decided that he would "defend himself" if anyone tried to remove him again. When Grether grabbed him the last time, Popp cut his throat with a knife. As the grim reality of what he had done set in, Popp told the Sheriff he was "ready to die."

Eyewitness Louis Hexamer also spoke with the media. He said that Popp was "not ugly when he came in," but after he started drinking he started to "get noisy" and Grether asked him to leave. Popp refused, so Grether physically removed him. When Popp returned the third time, "He had his hand in his pocket and I think must have had his knife open and ready for business," Hexamer said. "Grether went to put him out again when quick as a flash Popp had drawn the knife over Grether's throat." Popp ran, and Hexamer chased him. While in pursuit on foot, Hexamer saw police officer Isaac Harding, who continued chasing Popp. Hexamer returned to the saloon. "The scene was horrible," he said. "After being cut Grether lay in a pool of blood upon the saloon floor." Popp had struck his jugular vein, which caused blood to "spurt out in a terrifying manner." Bystanders helped carry Grether upstairs to his home above the saloon. The article continued, "Physicians were called and did all in their power to hold the fast ebbing spark of life; but useless were their efforts, for a half hour afterwards Grether breathed his last, and surrounded by his family and friends passed away." Services were planned for the afternoon of Saturday, April 5, with the German Odd Fellows, followed by interment at West Lawn Cemetery.

When the coroner arrived, he examined the wound. The *Repository* described it as "ghastly," saying, "[It] extended downward from behind the right ear through the skin, muscle and vein the sharp steel propelled by a strong and demon-inspired hand, had gone, stealing away life, a husband from his wife and a father from his children, all by a single stroke." Grether had five children, the oldest just twelve years old.

Popp was no stranger to the law. He had a rather lengthy police record of minor offenses, including the assault of a "cripple" named John Marx, a day laborer who worked for Nicholas Lehr, James Nighman, John Skeel and other contractors. Popp had never been married and had no children.

More details about what happened came out at the coroner's inquest. Jacob Zoellwer testified that Popp entered the saloon for the first time that day around 2:00 p.m. He was loud, but not angry. Grether asked him, "in a kind way," to be quiet. Grether then asked Zoellwer, Popp and others to help him carry whiskey barrels to the cellar and put them on the rack. Popp tapped all of the barrels for Grether, and all of the men were given a sample of whiskey. When they came back upstairs, Popp was again talking loudly, singing and drumming his hands on the bar. Shortly after Zoellwer left the saloon. Henry Lutz picked up the story from there, saying that Popp started a fight with a farmer, who said, "I have fed this man for two winters, and in the spring he always abuses me and goes away." Saying, "This is enough," Grether took Popp by the arm and escorted him out. Lutz said Popp returned shortly afterward and demanded another drink. Grether refused to serve him and again escorted him out.

August Albrecht testified that he stopped for a beer at Brobst's saloon on his way home from work at the Malleable Iron Works. On his way out, Popp stopped him and said, "That son of a b—— over there put me out twice, and I am going over again, and if he tries to put me out I will cut his throat." Albrecht headed in the direction of Grether's saloon to warn him, and Popp fell into step just behind him. They arrived at the same time, so Albrecht also witnessed the murder. Grether's wife testified that she did not think Popp had been in her husband's saloon before, or at least she had never seen him there. She didn't think he acted drunk at the time of the murder, because he was able to run on steady feet afterward. Grether's sister, Louisa, was helping to tend bar that day and said Popp's drinking had been "considerable," but he was not "very drunk."

The *Repository* described Popp as "a pitiful sight" on the morning of the inquest. He expressed regret about what had happened, adding that he wished he had "let whiskey alone, for it had undone him." He was worried about how his crime would affect his elderly father, who was living in Portage County. His mother had passed away several years earlier. "Popp looks the very picture of despair," the article said. "He is beginning to realize the enormity of his offense, but is bearing up as bravely as he can. He talked freely with the reporter, says he is inexpressibly sorry for his deed and that had he not been drunk at the time he would not now be occupying a murderer's cell." One week later, Popp was charged with first-degree murder. He entered a plea of not guilty.

Popp's trial was straightforward. It began on Monday, June 16, 1890, with jury selection. The following men were chosen: F.H. Linerode, Isaac Smith, A.H. Heighway, Abraham Baum, W.M.H. Ritt, Jess Zartman, Peter Kepplinger, William Holl, B.F. Trescott, David M. Kerstetter, William J. Putna and Orange Bissell. John C. Welty prosecuted the case, and Popp's defense attorney was A.L. Jones of Jones and Hudson. Judge Pease presided. Popp did not deny that he killed Grether, but his attorney argued that he was not guilty because he was intoxicated and therefore not responsible for his actions.

The saloon was crowded that day, so there were several people who witnessed the murder. The state called many of the same witnesses from the coroner's inquest, who all repeated the same story. Additional witnesses were called during the trial, who corroborated what the others had said. On cross-examination, the defense asked witnesses how much alcohol they saw Popp drink that day. Most had not paid attention to that and could not say one way or another.

In his testimony, Sherriff Krider recalled a conversation he had with Popp shortly after he was brought to the jail. "I went in and said, 'Popp what have you done,' and he said, 'I have cut him.' I said, 'You should not have used a knife,' and he said, 'I wanted revenge.' I said, 'I suppose you mean defend yourself,' and he said, 'No, revenge.' He said, 'he wanted to hear the band play and if Grether put him out he was going to have revenge.'" The sheriff testified on cross-examination that he didn't think Popp was "much intoxicated." The prosecution rested after just two days of testimony.

The first witnesses called by the defense spoke to Popp's good character. Henry Zimmer said that "when sober, he was peaceable and quiet." Conrad Reil said he was "quarrelsome sometimes" but was nice when he wasn't drinking. Under cross-examination, Reil admitted he had heard of "Popp fighting lots of times before that day." John Zelwer characterized Popp as "half drunk" on the afternoon of the murder. Some witnesses said they didn't talk to him enough to know if he was drunk or not, and some said he didn't seem drunk. Officer Harding recounted the story of his arrest and said Popp had been arrested previously for drunkenness. Some of the witnesses for the defense were called to raise questions about the reliability of the prosecution's witnesses, but with multiple people who saw the same thing, it was an ineffective strategy.

Judge Pease handed the case over to the jury on the morning of Friday, June 20, 1890. He reminded them that in a civil case, the weight of the evidence is the deciding factor, but in a criminal case, "where life or death is at stake, a higher degree of testimony is required in establishing the guilt of the defendant. Before a person can be found guilty, under a plea of not guilty, the jury must be fully satisfied beyond the existence of any reasonable doubt."

After taking four ballots over five and a half hours, at 2:30 p.m., the jury found Popp "guilty as charged in the indictment." They had not formally submitted whether they found him guilty of first-degree murder, second-degree murder or manslaughter, so Judge Pease sent them back into the jury room. They were only out of the courtroom for ten minutes before returning with a first-degree murder verdict. Upon returning to the jail, Turnkey Rigler said to Popp, "Well, Henry, they have given you the worst they could." He replied, in German, "Yes, but we have got to die sometime, anyhow."

Popp was sentenced to hang on October 22, 1890. Under a new state law, all executions were to take place at the state penitentiary. The sensational triple hanging in Canton a few years earlier had been a contributing factor to the decision to centralize executions, rather than having them take place in the communities in which the condemned was tried and convicted. Popp would be taken from Canton to Columbus within thirty days of the scheduled execution.

Popp was taken on his final journey to Columbus early on July 14, 1890. Over the next three months, all motions filed for a new trial or an appeal were denied. On the eve of his execution, the *Cincinnati Post* used derogatory dialect in its reporting of the German immigrant's final hours. Under the headline, "Dell Effrypody I Vas Sorry," the article said:

> *"I vas somedimes a hardt drinker," he goes on in a gentle, weak voice, "and when I haf the drinks I vas* [illegible]. *Bud I never ged indo drubbles pefore, andt but one dime I was arrested vor peint drunk. Id vas in Gandon* [Canton] *last April. I hadt peen drinkin all day, andt I vas in a haf tozen saloons maype, andt ven I ged roundt to Moritz Grether's saloon I vas a blum vool I dondt know. I dondt remember anydings aboudt id. I rememters moddings budt I vas in chail and my handts undt clodings vas ploody. I vas sorry!"*

In his final written confession, Popp did not deny killing Grether, whom he admitted he hadn't even met before that fateful day in his saloon.

Through the fuzzy haze of alcohol, he remembered the incident differently. He thought he was defending himself from Gerther's "rough" treatment of him as he was throwing him out the final time, which witnesses said did not happen. Popp blamed his intoxication for the murder, and he went to his grave believing that he should not have been convicted of murder in the first degree because he had no malice toward his victim. He said, "I do not want to die on the scaffold for crime of which I only have a faded and indistinct knowledge of committing, and I beg the community to intercede and save me from the awful fate of hanging. Though I have taken the life of a fellow man I am not bad at heart, and I ask that at least my life be spared."

Although Governor James E. Campbell had previously sent a telegram declining to intervene, just three hours before midnight on the day before the scheduled execution, he changed his mind. A new date was set for November 28. The State Board of Pardons denied Popp's petition on November 20, but again, at the last minute, Governor Campbell called off his execution. He had some doubts about whether Popp's crime was premeditated, and he wanted more time to consider his case. A new execution date was set for December 19. The night before his third execution date, Popp received word that the governor would not commute his sentence to life imprisonment after all. He was out of time.

The newspapers had portrayed Popp as an "ignorant immigrant," with very limited English, which initially garnered sympathy from the governor. But in the end, he wasn't buying it:

> *There is an error in this case which has been pretty well circulated through the press, and that is that Popp was a man of very great ignorance, a German who is unable to speak or understand the English language. I have, however, in my possession a letter written by him only yesterday, in a good hand, well spelled, and ordinarily grammatical, and to my mind this is evidence that he is a man above the average of intellectual capacity. I think he is more cunning than ignorant, and that his pretended dullness and stupidity, and want of knowledge of the English language have been parts of a plan to play upon the sympathies of the public and especially to appeal to his German fellow citizens. I have no hesitation whatever in refusing to interfere in this case, and though at one time, and before I examined it thoroughly I leaned very decidedly in his favor.*

Popp was one of two executions in the early morning hours of December 19. Elmer Sharkey, a Preble County man who had killed his mother, was hanged first, but his death did not come swiftly. The rope was not tied properly around his neck, so just after the warden pulled the lever of trap, the knot in the noose settled around his chin instead of his neck. "The crowd was horrified to see the body struggling," the *Repository* reported, "the hands working, the breast heaving and hear the most unearthly noises escape from the dying man's throat. The breath went through the windpipe with a sawing sound that was kept up for five minutes. Every face was blanched and strong men trembled as with palsy." Eventually, the struggling stopped, and Sharkey was pronounced dead.

Popp was next. It is unlikely that he was aware of what had happened to his fellow death row inmate. A new rope was put around his neck. When the warden pulled the level this time, death was almost immediate, and Popp became the first Stark County resident to die in the state penitentiary. His body was given to clergy, since his family did not claim him, and he was interred in Columbus.

7

ANNIE GEORGE

A s the dust was settling from the recent Spanish-American War, President William McKinley found himself dragged into a scandal back home in Canton when his brother-in-law, George D. Saxton, a prominent businessman, was found murdered in the front yard of his widowed lover's home on October 7, 1898. He was only forty-seven. He was widely known as a womanizer, and his jilted lover Annie George was immediately suspected.

The trouble began back in February 1892 when Sample C. George sued Saxton as the cause of the alienation of affections of his wife, Annie. The charge, as reported in the *Repository*, which was founded by Saxton's grandfather, claimed that "on March 1, 1889, in Canton, and on divers other days since that time in Canton and other places, Saxton wrongfully and wickedly debauched and carnally knew Anna E. George, she being the wife of the plaintiff, which fact Saxton knew." The charge continued that Anna "because infatuated in the defendant, so that, disregarding her duties toward the plaintiff and their two children, now ten and seven years of age, she abandoned the plaintiff, his home and family in November, 1889, and refuses to live with the plaintiff." The lawsuit claimed that Annie moved into a building owned by Saxton, where he also lived. Since he was "deprived of the fellowship, society and services of his wife and of her aid in his family and domestic affairs," George was suing Saxton for the exorbitant sum of $30,000.

Naturally, Saxton denied the affair. He said that the family had lived in rooms in the Saxton block in downtown Canton in 1888, and in the spring of 1890 Annie and another woman rented rooms in the same building as a headquarters for their dressmaking business. "During the terms of both leases my relations to these tenants were simply those of a landlord," he said.

Although the Saxton family no longer owned the *Repository*, it remained a rival newspaper to the *Stark County Democrat*, and George Saxton was a prominent businessman in town. William McKinley, a Republican, was governor of Ohio at the time, and Saxton was his wife's brother. Over the course of the lawsuit, the *Stark County Democrat* devoted much more ink to the story than the *Repository* did. In the first story that appeared in the *Stark County Democrat*, Saxton's statement was much longer:

> *My relations with Mrs. George have been simply those of landlord and tenant. I have had no other relations with her. She occupied rooms in the building with her husband for a long time and then they went away. She came back later but he did not come with her, they having had as I understood it, a misunderstanding. She opened up a dressmaking establishment and remained in the building until sometime last fall. She paid her rent and that is all the dealings I had with her. You may say that I have nothing to conceal in this matter and simply deny the allegations as you have stated them to me. I know nothing whatever about the case, consequently cannot give you any information. I never had any money dealings with the woman and simply deny the charge in toto.*

Additionally, the *Stark County Democrat* quoted Sample's lawyer, Nat C. McLean, who said, "He told me further that his wife had gone to Dakota and that she had been sent there by Mr. Saxton in order to get a divorce from him. He believed that she would try to get a divorce out there and then come back here and live with Mr. Saxton. He seemed determined and thought he had been greatly damaged."

On February 27, 1892, just weeks after George's lawsuit was made public, the *Repository* reported that Annie was indeed in Dakota and had started divorce proceedings against him on the charges of "extreme cruelty and abuse and that she left him and refused to live with him on account of fear of personal violence." Sheriff Krider served George with divorce papers. On August 4, the *Stark County Democrat* reported that Saxton was in Sioux Falls, South Dakota, "under sensational circumstances." Saxton said he made the trip to "secure depositions in defense of his suit." The article pointedly remarked that Annie's family was "very poor," yet she "seemed to have plenty of money on hand," which of course suggested that Saxton was supporting her. On October 6, under the headline "George-Saxton Scandal," the *Stark County Democrat* reported that a judge in Cleveland had dismissed the lawsuit. On February 5, 1895, the *Repository* reported that the lawsuit was back on the docket. It had been dismissed without prejudice, which meant that it could be refiled at a later date. Judge McCarty dismissed it again, this time because the statute of limitations had run out.

But Saxton's legal problems were far from over. On November 16, 1895, Annie started proceedings against him for "the recovery of [an] appended list of household goods alleged to be detained and held by him and the property of the plaintiff." The next day, the *Repository* reported that the police had been called to Saxton's office because Annie showed up demanding to speak to him. "This was positively refused," the article said, "and the woman remained in the building. She was eventually escorted out by Officer Rohn." Saxton filed a "general denial to all allegations" via his attorney James J. Grant as reported on January 28, 1896. On March 31, the *Repository* reported that "all suits and counter suits" between Annie and George had been settled out of court. One of the lawsuits was reportedly a "breach of contract" suit she filed against him for $50,000, in which she claimed that he had promised to marry her after her divorce was final but then refused to follow through.

For more than a year, things were quiet between them, at least in the newspapers, until the *Stark County Democrat* broke the story that George and Annie were at it again. This time, she was sending him letters threatening to kill him. Under the headline "Annoying Him," the August 19, 1897 edition of the newspaper said, "From reports which have reached this city by way of Cleveland, it would appear that George D. Saxton has tired of the attentions being paid him by Mrs. Anna George, and has determined to place her where she cannot annoy him further." The article said that Annie's letter made "all sorts of demands and, so those declare who have seen the letters, using such language and threats as is prohibited by the postal authorities. The matter was allowed to proceed for a time, according to a friend of Saxton, who relates the occurrences, but it finally became unbearable. The episode of the little wheeling [bicycling] excursion, which was given to the public recently, served as a vehicle for Saxton to warn the woman that he did not desire her attentions, but it is said that he has since received a letter which could readily be made the basis of an action against the writer for sending forbidden matter through the mails." The situation was being handled in Cleveland, and George did not want to be interviewed locally. Although the letters were unsigned, a warrant was issued for Annie's arrest. The *Stark County Democrat* quoted a Cleveland newspaper article: "She is said to have threatened his lady friends, and on several occasions insulted Mr. Saxton in public. The woman is very specific in the means with which she threatens to revenge herself. She tells Mr. Saxton in her letters that she carries a Smith & Wesson revolver, a large knife and other weapons. It is reported that her motives are a mixture of love and revenge." At some point, George got a restraining order against her for the entire Saxton block.

On December 2, 1897, the *Stark County Democrat* reported that Sample George's lawsuit against Saxton was back in the courts. The circuit court had reversed the decision of the lower court, which had agreed that the statute of limitations had expired because more than five years had lapsed. Annie's now ex-husband was still suing for $20,000. He claimed that George had paid all of Annie's expenses for her trip to South Dakota to obtain a divorce from him. William R. Day, who was now assistant secretary of state, was one of George's attorneys in the case. The state supreme court affirmed the decision of circuit court and remanded the case back to the common pleas court in Stark County. On March 24, the *Stark County Democrat* reported that Saxton's lawyers, James J. Grant and Judge Day, filed an answer to the case pleading a "general denial" of all wrongdoing. Curiously, the reappearance of this case was never reported in the *Repository*. On October 6, the *Stark County Democrat* reported that the case had been settled out of court, noting that the defendant "has always appeared indifferent." George agreed to pay Annie's ex-husband $1,825 and would cover all court costs. After the settlement was reached, Annie's ex-husband announced that he had been happily remarried for over a year and he had accepted much less than his original lawsuit because he feared his new marriage would negatively influence the jury if the case went to trial. Annie knew nothing about his marriage until it was revealed in the coverage of the court case.

GEORGE D. SAXTON SHOT.

Death Came to Him Instantaneously, Before the Arrival of People Attracted By the Reports.

MRS. ANNIE E. GEORGE UNDER ARREST.

The Tragedy Occurred in Lincoln Avenue, in Front Of the Residence of Mrs. Eva B. Althouse, Where Mr. Saxton Had Called—Four or Five Shots Fired—Three Took Effect—Mrs. George Reported to Have Been In the Vicinity.

Headline: "George D. Saxton Shot." This headline announcing George Saxton's murder appeared in the *Repository* on October 8, 1898. Annie George was immediately suspected and arrested within hours of the murder. *Courtesy of the* Repository.

Drawing of Annie, Mrs. Althouse and the scene. George Saxton was murdered in the front yard of Eva B. Althouse's home at 319 Lincoln Avenue NW in Canton. When the trial began, the *Repository* printed this drawing of the house, including portraits of Annie, George's jilted lover and accused killer, and Eva, his widowed girlfriend. *Courtesy of the* Repository.

The very next day, George Saxton was murdered in the front yard of Eva B. Althouse's home at 319 Lincoln Avenue NW. Annie was immediately arrested. The *Repository* said that George had left his brother-in-law M.C. Barber's home on his bicycle around 6:00 p.m. At 6:10 p.m., neighbors heard four or five gunshots. Four bullets entered the victim, and he was killed instantly. Althouse's home was locked and dark, and neighbors said she had not been home for three days. She had been staying at her brother's home on North Walnut Street, taking care of her sister-in-law who was gravely ill. The article continued, "Another neighbor volunteered the information that the woman who had done the shooting had gone to the rear of the premises, which is away from the center of the city. The description of the woman was that of a tall woman in a dark gossamer or other wrap, and in details tallied close to that of the woman arrested. Mrs. George, the suspect, could not be found at her late residence, having moved Thursday. She was heard of at an uptown restaurant at 4:45 and some time later a motorman said he left her off a car at Hazlett Avenue, the street next to that on which Mrs. Althouse lives."

Annie was arrested around 8:00 p.m. She had recently rented a room from Mrs. Jacob Oberlin, after shipping her belongings to her mother's home in Hanoverton in Columbiana County. Mrs. Oberlin told investigators that Annie had left at 9:00 a.m. and had not returned. While they were interviewing Oberlin, police saw Annie walking near the home. The *Repository* said, "When she was taken into the station she was sweating profusely, but seemed to be as calm and self-possessed as at any time in her life. She had on a black dress, white sailor hat with a white veil. She carried a dark colored shoulder cape trimmed with fur." She refused to answer when prosecuting attorney Atlee Pomerene asked her where she was at six o'clock on the night she was arrested and if she knew that George was dead. "I notice there are a great many burs on your dress," he said. "Will you tell where you got them?" The article said, "Not a muscle of Mrs. George's face moved and her head did not move a particle to see whether there were any burs on her dress, as the prosecutor said." Her hands were scraped, and officials planned to look for any traces of gunpowder. Dr. Maria C. Pontius was called to the jail to search Annie before she was put in a cell. No weapons were found.

President McKinley was hosting a reception in the White House that evening, and his aides withheld the news for two hours. At 10:00 p.m., while the president was shaking hands and chatting with his guests, Secretary Porter tapped him on the shoulder and took him aside to tell him the news. "He could scarcely believe the words which fell from the secretary's lips," said the *Repository*. "For a full instant he stood with his head bowed and his face white. Then he turned and whispered a few words in Secretary Porter's ear and hastened to the side of Mrs. McKinley, whom he had left alone to receive the guests. Not a word of what had happened was said to her." The president gently broke the news to her later that night. Funeral arrangements were not made until President and Mrs. McKinley confirmed when they could return to Canton.

There were several witnesses in the area who spoke to the *Repository*, including Henry Bederman, who was in a grocery store nearby. He said he heard two shots and saw the flash from the gun. "I went immediately to the door of the store and after about two minutes had been elapsed, I heard two more. Before I heard these, however, I saw a woman or someone dressed in woman's clothes, go away from the Althouse steps, rather slowly, then turn around and go back again. At that time I heard two more shots. This time the woman started to run." Mrs. Althouse told the *Repository* that she could not understand why George was at her house, because he knew she was not home. She added, "I wish to say this: that there have been reports circulated that he used to come up to my house, not coming up directly through Tuscarawas street. This is not so. During the time I have been going with him, he always came right up in a straightforward manner. He has always been very kind to me, and has always used me well. I feel very badly over his death. If I had known that this trouble between Mr. Saxton and Mrs. George would culminate in this manner, I would not have gone with him. I tried at one time to put an end to it, fearing that she would carry out some of her threats, but he said he knew she would do nothing, so I thought it would be unfair to stop going with him after that. I never dreamed she would really do anything of this kind."

Officials spent most of Saturday looking for a murder weapon, to no avail. The coroner's inquest began late Saturday afternoon. Mrs. Oberlin testified that when Annie was told she was under arrest, she only said, "Well!" She did not ask for what reason she was under arrest and did not say anything else. Grocer Joseph A. Lippert said he was in front of his store on West Tuscarawas Street, purchasing celery from a woman with a cart, around 8:30 p.m., when he saw Annie walk by. "There goes Mrs. George," he said, "the woman who is supposed to have shot George Saxton, and it is kind of funny for her to be coming down this way when everybody is looking for her in the west end." He said she was wearing a dark colored dress and was walking "leisurely along." Chase Rittenhouse, the streetcar driver, told the inquest that when Annie boarded the car, a passenger sitting toward the front told him who it was. He said she got off at Hazlett Avenue, just a few streets away from the scene of the crime, at around 5:55 p.m. "She didn't ring the bell," he said. "I stopped the car for someone else to get off." He didn't notice what she was wearing or which way she walked.

Henry Bederman added more information than what he had shared with the newspaper. "Before she went back the second time he called 'help!' It was awful low and we could just hear it across the street," he said. "It seemed that the woman heard him call and came back and fired the second shots. I did not hear any talking before the shots were fired." Although he maintained he saw a woman, he could not identify who it was. It was extremely dark outside, and he had to strike a match to provide enough light to identify the victim.

Meanwhile, Annie talked "freely enough concerning other matters" but would say "absolutely nothing" about the murder. The *Repository* reported that several months earlier, she had pointed a gun at George's chest, but he was close enough to grab her arm. The next morning, she reportedly said, "I will not stand by and see George Saxton going with this woman. He has promised to marry me just as soon as my former husband's case against him is settled and if he fails to keep that promise I will kill him. I'll do it if I hang the next day, but I do not think any jury on earth would convict me after hearing my story."

On Monday morning, Annie was charged with first-degree murder and pleaded not guilty. She entered the courtroom wearing a gray plaid skirt and brightly colored shirtwaist, with a "jaunty hat trimmed in the season's style." She remained completely calm. She retained Mayor James A. Rice as her attorney, forcing Justice Jacob Reinger to fill the role of acting mayor with regard to her case. Rice issued a statement to the Canton police department that his role in the case should have no impact on the officers performing their duties, for both sides of the case. Annie also hired attorneys John C. Welty and James A. Sterling, who would ultimately defend her in court. An elevator operator reported that she had visited Sterling's office around 7:00 p.m. on the night of the murder, although he was not in at the time.

George's funeral was held Monday afternoon. Naturally, given the high profile of his famous sister and brother-in-law, George's murder was front-page news across the country. The Canton telegraph office was flooded with messages of condolence from around the world. Locals stopped the president on the street to offer their sympathies. There was a crowd at the train station when they arrived Monday morning. As the president and first lady made their way from the train to the carriage that was waiting for them, "the crowd with heads uncovered and bowed, silently opened a passage way through which they passed. Mrs. McKinley was supported by the arm of the President who gave that close kindly attention to her comfort so characteristic of him." Close friends and family gathered at the Saxton home for the funeral. The service, led by Reverend O.B. Milligan of the First Presbyterian Church, was short and simple. Afterward, George's loved ones accompanied his body to West Lawn Cemetery in a procession of carriages, led by President and Mrs. McKinley. He was laid to rest very close to where he had been killed. His pallbearers were some of Canton's most prominent men: Judge George E. Baldwin, Hon. William A. Lynch, George B. Frease, J.H. Kenny and attorneys David B. Smith and James J. Grant.

Many of the witnesses who had testified at the coroner's inquest also testified at the preliminary hearing, which began on Tuesday afternoon. Having consulted with the McKinley and Barber families, it was decided that the court proceedings should be carried out in a normal timeline, not expedited in any way. Officer Fred McCloud, who was one of the men who arrested Annie, said he smelled gunpowder on her right hand and found burs on her dress. Officer Henry Piero corroborated his fellow officer's observations, adding that he observed burs and Spanish needles on her dress, both of which were found in the vacant lot next to the Althouse residence. Under cross-examination, Annie's lawyers asked both police officers if they had searched for Mrs. Althouse the night of the murder. Both said they had not. Later, the state would try to enter the Spanish needles and burrs into evidence, but they were excluded.

Perry Van Horne, a reporter for the *Stark County Democrat*, was the next person to testify. He said that several months earlier, Annie had sent for him because she wanted the story of her "trouble" with George reported in the newspaper. He said she told him she had met George at the Althouse home and pulled a gun on him. "She said she would shoot Saxton if he did not keep his promise with her and marry her after the settlement of the case of her husband against Mr. Saxton," he said. "That case was settled last Wednesday afternoon." He said he visited Annie in jail and asked her if she remembered telling him this. She said "nothing audible but, with closed lips assented with a nod of the head."

The defense chose an unlikely person as its only witness—Mrs. Althouse. She said she had received a letter from Annie, which she had given to Saxton as part of his lawsuit against her. She said the letter was unsigned, but she knew it was from Annie based on previous conversations. "I never talked to Mrs. George, but once," she said. "She stood outside my house and talked to me on several occasions, but I did not answer her." Althouse said she and George Saxton had talked about getting married, although they were not engaged. On cross-examination, the prosecution asked her about the content of the letters. "She would cut my heart out if she caught me with Saxton," she said. "She told me by word of mouth that she would kill me. She molested me by coming to my house and daring me to come out of the house. She threatened me and called me names. She was at my house very often. One time I was with Mr. Saxton and I saw her and I dropped my wheel [bicycle] and ran to the house, leaving Mrs. George with Saxton." She said that Saxton had a key to her home because he would water her plants and feed her bird when she was away.

Next, both sides gave closing arguments. Annie's attorneys argued that there was no direct evidence to link her with the crime. She was on the streets that evening, but that was "nothing out of the ordinary." Prosecuting attorney Pomerene said he would "expect the same statements from the defense if the accused had been seen in the act of the murder." He said that the point of the preliminary hearing was to establish if there were "reasonable grounds to believe the accused committed that crime." He said her behavior at the police station "spoke louder than words. If she had been on legitimate business she could have explained it and would have been released. But she chose to keep her mouth shut. She said she would kill George Saxton, and with almost lightning rapidity she keeps her word. The case was settled Wednesday and on Friday evening George Saxton was a corpse." Welty responded by saying that no one actually saw Annie shoot him, adding, "The murder might have been committed in self-defense for all we know." Judge Reigner decided there was a "chain of circumstances connecting Mrs. George with the crime" and the case would go to a grand jury.

After several months of fruitless attempts to have her case dismissed, Annie's trial began on April 4, 1899, with great fanfare. The entire first day was consumed with "technicalities and formalities." Annie made a rather grand entrance, dressed to the nines. "She wore a close-fitting, stylish costume of light blue storm serge, with a plaited silk yoke of lighter blue and a collar of blue ribbon," said the *Repository*. "She wore a stylish hat of medium size, trimmed in small black plumes, large black wings, black ribbon and steel ornaments with a small cluster of white flowers. A black feather boa was thrown loosely around her neck. Her hands were gloved in dark brown kids. She greeted her counsel cordially, and gave undivided attention to the proceedings, watching the court intently." A looming concern was

Stark County Court House, Judge Taylor's Court Room, Where George Case Is Being Tried Is Just Over the Portico on the Right (Market Street) Side Of the Building

Courthouse drawing. On April 16, 1899, the *Repository* printed a drawing of the Stark County Court House, pointing out the exact location of the courtroom in which Annie George's trial was taking place. *Courtesy of the* Repository.

the fact that Mrs. Althouse could not be located to testify, although it was rumored that officials knew her whereabouts, but she could not be called as a witness as long as she was not in Ohio. She was not in contempt of court, because she had not been served a subpoena. More than 150 witnesses received subpoenas from the prosecution or the defense. Each witness

CONSPICUOUS PERSONAGES AT THE TRIAL OF MRS. GEORGE.

Annie with Welty, Judge Taylor and Atlee Pomerene. Throughout her trial, Annie George was dressed fashionably in the courtroom. The *Repository* printed portraits of some of the key players in the courtroom drama, including her attorney John C. Welty, Judge Taylor and Atlee Pomerene, prosecuting attorney. Joseph Kline, who was convicted of poisoning his father in 1881, had briefly studied law with Welty. *Courtesy of the* Repository.

received one dollar a day from the day they registered with the clerk until they were excused. The *Stark County Democrat* noted, "Murder trials…are always expensive, and this one no doubt will cost the county a pretty figure."

The *Stark County Democrat*'s coverage of the trial's opening was reported under the headline "After Months of Preparation the Trial of the Handsome

Woman, Whose Life Was Wrecked by Saxton, Is Begun Before an Able Jurist, Eminently Qualified to Protect the Interests of Both State and Defendant." Based on the defense's opening statement, the article dissected George Saxton's character, asserting that he was popular with women but not exactly well liked by men. "That he deliberately and systematically set about to wreck more families than one is confidently believed by many citizens of this city who know his history," the article said. "Scandals began to find their way among the people, and George Saxton became an outcast from society, ostracized by the circles that formerly knew him, avoided by former friends of the male sex and shunned by good women who had formerly welcomed him to their homes." Annie was described as a "beautiful, attractively-shaped, big-hearted country woman." George was characterized as a spider who laid a trap for Annie, a fair butterfly. The article charged that he began to woo her with dresses and jewelry and told her that the only thing holding her back from being a society lady was her humble husband. So she left him for the "well-bred landlord of the Saxton block." But their happiness was short-lived, as "it was the same old tale with Saxton." He soon tired of her. Next came all the lawsuits. The article concluded with the noncommittal notion that Annie's guilt would be proven or disproven as the trial progressed.

The first day of testimony was taken up with medical witnesses explaining how Saxton had died and where each bullet entered his body, to establish that the deceased had, in fact, been murdered. James Shetler repeated his testimony from the preliminary trial, stating that he saw Annie George get off the streetcar at Hazlett Avenue. He said he did not remember exactly what she was wearing but thought maybe she was not dressed in black. J.A. Shanafelt was also on the streetcar and remembered seeing Annie get off at Hazlett. He said she was wearing a black dress and carried a wrap that was either black or dark blue. On cross-examination of every witness associated with the streetcar line, Annie's attorneys tried to establish that the streetcars were running late that night, which would have made it impossible for her to be at the murder scene at the time George was killed.

On Tuesday afternoon, the attorneys "locked horns on a legal proposition" regarding whether or not testimony that Annie refused to answer any questions could be used against her. The state argued that her conduct could be considered the equivalent of a confession, while the defense said she was "under duress" as a prisoner and therefore no conversation or silence should be admissible. Judge Taylor ruled that witnesses could not testify about her refusal to answer any questions, based on the fact that if the accused chooses not to take the stand on his or her own behalf, by state law that was not to be considered damaging to his or her case. It was the first of many victories for Annie's attorneys, who would continue to press for key evidence to be excluded from the case.

Judge T.T. McCarty testified that about forty minutes before the murder, Annie showed up at his house, asking if she could go to the Saxton block. He told her that the restraining order was still in place, so she could not go there. She told him that Saxton had promised to "have the injunction dissolved," but Judge McCarty had not heard anything about it. "That is like some of his other promises," she said. She said she wanted to see George, and the judge suggested she send a note to ask for a meeting. "She did not know whether he would meet her and asked if she could go to his house. I said, 'No, Mrs. George, you had better leave Saxton alone.' She replied, 'I will not go; I do not want to disobey any of the rules of the court.'" Then she left.

On Wednesday, Officer Piero testified that the substance found on Annie's right hand smelled to him like gunpowder. He also said that three burdocks or "burrs" and forty or fifty Spanish needles were removed from her skirt. The defense theorized that perhaps the burrs Officer Piero saw on Annie's skirts had been transferred from his own pants to her skirt as he walked next to her after her arrest. Later Officer Rohn testified that Spanish needles and burdocks were "numerous in the vacant lot near the Althouse place." Upon cross-examination, Welty asked the officer if he had any burrs on his uniform after he searched the vacant lot. He did not but suggested that a woman "takes a wider path than a man." Welty responded that a woman would hold up her skirts while passing through an area that was overgrown with weeds.

Next, Officer Dickerhoff testified that on the night before the murder, Annie had asked him to go to the Saxton block to look for George, because she was not allowed to go there herself. She said she wanted him to be with her in case she did see Saxton, because she was afraid of him. On cross-examination, Sterling asked Officer Dickerhoff if Annie had told him that George had kicked her down the stairs the last time she had gone to see him. He said yes, she had.

Next, W.F. Cook, who was nearly completely deaf, testified that he in the spring of 1897, he had seen Annie at the top of the stairs in the building where he lived. She was holding a gun. Her attorneys objected, because the incident had happened too long ago, but the witness was allowed to continue. He said she hid it under her wrap and never said anything to him. On June 1, 1899, he said he saw George and Mrs. Althouse at Meyers Lake. Annie was watching them from about forty feet away.

On Thursday, April 13, Annie's former attorney W.O. Werntz took the stand. When asked about a conversation he had with Annie, he initially refused to answer, citing attorney-client privilege. Judge Taylor considered the issue and ruled that once a conversation shifted to the contemplation of a crime, privilege rights ceased. He said on the Monday before the murder, which was later determined to have been several weeks before that on cross-examination, Annie told him she had a .38-caliber revolver that she had purchased in Chicago, but she did not say what she was going to do with it. When discussing the lawsuit between George and her ex-husband, Annie said, "When the suit of Sample C. George is settled there will be a funeral or a wedding." Then he said, "She asked what effect it would have on the suit if she killed Saxton. I told her the result might be the same, but if she was going to kill him she had better wait until the case was settled. She said if she shot him she would make a good job of it. [She] would give him all the balls she had." She asked if it would be a good plan to have two revolvers—one to shoot him with and another to leave with his body. Werntz said, "I told her, in view of the threats she had made against Saxton, no one would believe she had killed him in self-defense." This last answer was objected to and stricken from the record. Ultimately, Werntz said he advised her to leave Saxton alone.

On cross-examination, Annie's lawyers were able to build their own case about how George had wronged her. They did not want the jury to hear about her threats, but once Werntz was allowed to testify, they used it to their advantage. Werntz said that she did tell him about George's failure to keep his promise to marry her, and that he was the "only man she loved." He said, "She said Saxton had been after her for years to leave her husband before she consented to do so. She told me a number of places where they had stopped together and registered as husband and wife." He also said that when she lived in the Saxton block, he stayed with her in her rooms at night. His testimony also revealed that Saxton had paid her expenses for a year while she was living in Cleveland; Saxton also promised to give both of Annie's sons property in Canton and that he would continue to support her until they could be married. On re-direct, Pomerene asked if she had discussed the possible penalty she might receive for killing George. After the defense's objection was overruled, Werntz answered, "She said that if she would not get more than ten years in the penitentiary she would kill him or shoot him." (He could not recall the exact term she used.)

The next witness, Mary Finley, had rented a room in the Saxton block and also heard Annie make threats. In September or October 1897, Finley said Annie told her, "Just wait till the case of Sample C. George and Saxton is settled. I'll see Saxton. I'm going to ask Mayor Rice to go with me to Saxton's office. I'm going to ask Saxton what he will do for me and if he does nothing I'll shoot him so full of lead that he will stand still." Finley told her not to do it, because she would be sent to prison. Annie replied, "Only a few years, what's that." Finley also testified that she wanted a man named Harry Clark to buy her a gun. In February 1898, she said she was teasing Annie that George was going to marry Mrs. Althouse, to which she responded, "Just wait till that suit with Sample is settled, I'll fix him. I'll not do it like a coward. I'll go up in front of him and let him know who did it."

On cross-examination, Welty pelted her with questions, causing Finley to show "evidence of confusion." She admitted that she had spoken to the opposing counsel about what she was going to say on the stand. On Friday morning, Annie's attorneys asked the judge to prevent the prosecution from discussing the case with the witnesses, but the judge said there was no law about that. Cross-examination continued, and Finley said she had gone to Pomerene's office, but she was not instructed on what to say.

Next, Mary Nauman testified that Annie told her in August 1897 that she "went out to the Althouse home and sat on a neighbor's porch till Saxton and Mrs. Althouse rode up on their wheels. Mrs. Althouse went into the house and Mrs. George with a pistol in her hand made him come away with her. When she dropped the pistol Saxton picked it up. At the Tuscarawas Street bridge she asked him if he wanted to die then. He walked on and said nothing. Mrs. George said she could have killed him then, but she wanted Sample George to get some of his money first." Nauman also said Annie told her she had written an unsigned, "ugly threatening letter." Annie also told her "if Saxton didn't marry her after he settled with Sample George he would not walk the streets of Canton another day. She would walk right up to him and shoot him, and she would make a good job of it. She said, 'Let them prove it.'" Nauman, like Finley, told her not to do it, and Annie replied that she "always got out of trouble and would get out of this." On cross-examination, Sterling recounted many of the stories told by Werntz about how George had treated Annie and asked her if she had heard each one. She replied no every time. The next witness, Nettie McAllister, repeated much of the testimony that had already been said by other witnesses. But she also testified that Annie had told her that she had never loved her husband. "She said she never liked him from the day she married him," McAllister said.

On Friday afternoon, testimony regarding the chemical analysis of the alleged gunpowder sample taken from Annie's right hand was excluded.

It was a controversial decision that seemed to be at odds with established precedent. Judge Taylor arrived at his ruling on the technicality that Annie did not provide the sample voluntarily, and the sample itself was not sufficient for chemical analysis. The judge said that it was not lawful to cut a suspect's hair or pull their teeth for evidence, so the burden was on the state to prove that Annie had voluntarily supplied the cuticle sample to Dr. Maria Pontius. The prosecution did not believe this action would weaken its case, because previous witnesses had already established that in their opinion, the substance on her hand was gunpowder. The defense was pleased to be able to get Annie's grievances against George heard by the jury, from the prosecution's own witnesses.

Perry Van Horne, the former *Stark County Democrat* reporter who had testified at the preliminary hearing, repeated his testimony that Annie wanted a story written about Saxton "to roast him a little." He said Annie told him he was "not treating her right. He was running around with other women when he had promised to marry her." Next, Mary E. Grabel testified that in February 1896, Annie had told her, "Saxton had ruined her life and if he did not marry her she would riddle his body with bullets." On cross-examination, Welty asked her if she was addicted to opium, which she denied, but she did admit to purchasing some on the recommendation of her doctor for a chronic illness.

Next, the defense objected to the qualifications of Michael Bar, a money order clerk at the post office, who claimed he knew Annie's handwriting and could identify it on the threatening unsigned letter. The *Repository* said, "The letter is said to be a tirade of threats and abuse of Saxton, claimed to have been written by Mrs. George. Another effort will probably be made to identify it." Later in the trial, Bar was recalled, and it was established that he was competent to identify Annie's handwriting. But the content of the letter was not admitted, because Bar disclosed he had only seen the envelope, not the letter itself. Judge Taylor said there was no evidence that Annie had written the letter, nor that it had actually been sent.

Next, the state claimed it had two eyewitnesses who could place Annie at the scene of the crime: the grocer's wife, Christina Eckroate, and her daughter Laura Huwig. Eckroate said she was at the supper table when she heard the first shots and in her bedroom when she heard the second shots. "I took the screen out of the window and leaned out," she said. "I saw a person stooping forward and saw two flashes of a revolver fired by the stooping figure. The shots seemed to be fired towards the ground. The person walked slowly away. Then she turned back and stooped as if to pick something up. Then the person turned away again. I went to my lawn and saw the person walking towards the vacant lot. When she reached it she began to run and disappeared through the lot." She was asked who it was, to which she replied, "It was Mrs. George." The defense objected and was overruled. Eckroate said there was light on the street from the widows in the grocery and from the front windows of another house. On cross-examination, Welty asked her if she talked to Annie. She said she did not. She also admitted that she didn't tell anyone she thought she saw Annie until she heard the prosecution was building their case. She said there were some leaves on the trees, but she had cleaned up the yard several times before that night. She said she "recognized the figure by its form." Then Welty began his campaign to discredit the witness. "In direct testimony she was clear and concise," the *Repository* said, "and in cross-examination apparent inconsistencies could readily be explained by failure to comprehend the language of the questions asked her by those observing her manner. She did, however, clearly and frankly say in this cross-examination that she is addicted to the morphine habit and that she had been for the past nine or ten years. But this has not disqualified her from performing her usual household duties."

Next, her daughter, Mrs. Huwig, took the stand. She said that after she heard the shots, she went out to the gate and saw "a form facing north and the shots were fired north. I saw a form walk down to the corner of the first vacant lot. Then the form returned to where I first saw it. This was at the Althouse steps. The form stooped down and then turned away and ran through the vacant lot south of the place. As she turned around she faced the grocery store." She described the form as tall and slender. As the state tried to establish that the form she saw was Annie, several objections were sustained. Eventually, the witness was able to say that Annie resembled the form she saw. On cross-examination, Sterling got her to say that she could not swear that the form she saw was a woman, only that it was wearing women's clothes.

Next, J.G. Best provided an alibi for Mrs. Althouse, who had still not been found to testify. He said she was at his home from five o'clock to seven that evening. There was no cross-examination, although the defense moved to have the evidence excluded and was overruled.

The state then called William J. Hasler, a former police officer, who said he searched the neighborhood on October 10 and found a revolver under a log on the northeast corner of South and High Streets. He took it home and hid it until January 10. Portions of his story were excluded, including that he had been told by Mayor Rice, who was one of Annie's lawyers at the time, where to find the gun; that he had been sent to find and dispose of the gun; and that he lied to the mayor, saying he did not find it. He said that he went to see Annie in the jail, and said, "I have found the revolver you hid at the corner of South and High streets. The one Rice sent me for. What shall I do with it? She said I should see Mr. Welty about it and then see me again." The gun was shown to the witness, who identified it as the one he had found. It was established that it was a .38-caliber, which was the same caliber as the bullets that had been removed from George's body.

Under cross-examination, Welty accused him of being a paid witness on behalf of the state. He asked if he had wanted the county commissioners to offer a reward to him for finding the gun, which he denied. Welty asked if he had testified before the grand jury. He had not but said that Pomerene knew the story and did not ask him to testify. Hasler admitted that he had been a candidate for the Democratic nomination for marshal, and he wanted to keep the story quiet until after the election for fear it would hurt his campaign. He said, "Rice would have hurt me. I would have been out of job." Welty again accused him of being a paid witness. "I said I would lose my job if I gave up the gun. Mr. Pomerene said he had authority to pay me under such circumstances if I wanted it. I do not want pay and am not now being paid or under promise of being paid."

On Monday, the state called Mary Glick, who testified that she looked out her window after she heard the shots. There was a lamp burning in her window, which faced the Althouse residence. She said she had been to the Eckroate residence that morning specifically to see if she could see the Althouse steps from Mrs. Eckroate's bedroom window. She said that she could. Upon cross-examination, Welty recalled that he and Sterling had gone to her house the previous week to test what could be seen from her window. "You put the lamp where it was the night of the death?" She had. "We tested what could be seen from across the street and you said you could recognize anyone?" She replied, "No sir, you are trying to make me say what I didn't say." Welty said, "Didn't Brother Sterling put a handkerchief on his head so we could see him?" She replied, "You didn't ask me to recognize him. You asked me if I could see the handkerchief, and I could."

As soon as the state rested its case, the defense recalled some of the state's witnesses. The cross-examination seemed to indicate that Annie's defense might be "emotional insanity," although it was not stated in so many words. Werntz, Annie's former lawyer, was first. He said during the conversations he had previously related, she had appeared flushed and excited and, at times, angry, aggravated or nervous. The defense tried to get Charles Frazer to say that the night of the murder was so dark he needed a lantern to find his lost hat. He said he did not.

Next, the defense had a number of depositions from witnesses in the west that they wanted to read. The state objected, saying, "The state could accede a possible relevancy if insanity was the defense," he said, "but no such defense had been set up. A plea of not guilty of the homicide had been entered and that was what the state had been called upon to meet." Judge Taylor allowed the depositions on the grounds that showing the relationship between the accused and the victim was "proper."

Through a written deposition, a South Dakota hotel operator named Charles M. Seeley testified that Annie had stayed at his hotel during the winter of 1892–93. He said George Saxton had come for one week, and his room was on the same floor as hers. They had been seen eating their meals together, but there was nothing unusual about their conduct. He said that Annie paid her bill each week and always had money. Oscar K. Brown testified that he had cashed checks for her that were written by Saxton, and Charles E. Judd testified that he saw Annie and George enter the same room. When he checked the guest register, he saw that that room was assigned to "George Saxton and wife."

On Wednesday, the court ruled that the defense could not present witnesses who would introduce the names of other women in connection with George, except for Mrs. Althouse, which meant a number of the defense witnesses could not be called. Thomas Shepard, who had been a janitor in the Saxton block, testified that when George was out of town, he had let Annie into his office and she took the contents of his wastepaper basket. On cross-examination, he said that before he placed a restraining order upon her, Annie would often stay in the hallway for hours at a time outside George's door. Under re-direct, Shepard was not allowed to answer if she was there to try to get her belongings that George was withholding from her.

Next, Dr. Douglass Swartz testified that the night in question was so dark he had trouble finding a house he was called to visit. He said that "a person could not have been recognized at a distance of more than three or four feet." Under cross-examination, Pomerene suggested that most of his bicycle ride had taken place under electric streetlights, and perhaps his vision on the unilluminated side streets had not fully adjusted to the darkness. He denied that artificial light had affected his eyesight to that degree. Next, Charles Summers testified that he had seen Mrs. Althouse at Saxton's rooms frequently, "at most any hour," and on Monday morning he would "remove dishes and bottles from which they had evidently eaten." He also said he had frequently seen other women in the halls visiting, but Sterling did not attempt to get him to name any names. Under cross-examination, Pomerene suggested he ran a gambling operation, which he denied. He admitted that Saxton had "talked cross to me" so he had quit, but he had worked for him three times after that.

Next, Welty tried to show that as part of her housekeeping duties, Lena Lindeman had seen revolvers in his rooms. The state objected, and the court asked why Welty brought up this line of questions. "We expect to show that he had revolvers and carried them, that it may have had something to do with the affair on Lincoln Avenue." The judge asked if he planned to connect it that way, and he replied, "We cannot say that." The court ruled that he could not continue that line of questioning. Lindeman testified that Annie had been at her house from 12:00 p.m. to 5:30 p.m. She said she had taken her hat and coat when she arrived, and there was no revolver in either. "I was ironing Saxton's clothes during the afternoon," she said. "Mrs. George took the tidies and trimmed the ragged edges. She knew the tidies were Saxton's and said she had worked them" when she was in South Dakota with him. She told Linderman that George had settled with her ex-husband and that she expected to be married soon. "She said she loved him and she did not believe he would go back on his promise to marry her." She said she had looked closely at Annie's dress, because she had said she was going to give it to her after her marriage. She said if she had hidden a revolver, she would have seen it. Additionally, she said that Annie went into the backyard a number of times, and there were Spanish needles and burrs in the yard, although under cross-examination she said she didn't notice any on her clothes when she left. In an effort to discredit Mrs. Eckroate's testimony, Sterling persuaded Charles Frazer to testify that he had spoken with her about her morphine habit. Later, the defense called Dr. J.C. Eyman of Cleveland to testify about the effects of morphine. He said, "One of the first results after a person has become addicted to the habit is the loss of honor and truthfulness and that the subject retains little or no principle." Pomerene cross-examined the witness, saying, "Is not untruthfulness in those addicted to the habit largely confined to efforts to get the drugs?" He said yes, but it was not limited to that. On redirect, the doctor said he had 1,050 insane patients under his care and 50 to 100 of them had become insane from using opium. Later in the case, Mrs. Eckroate's husband was recalled and testified that he knew she took morphine, it had affected her memory negatively and recently it had been getting worse.

The defense then called a series of witnesses who testified that there were burrs and possibly Spanish needles in several other locations where Annie could have been that evening. Some also testified as to the darkness of the night. Some witnesses said they couldn't tell for sure if the figure leaving the scene was a woman or a man. Shepard was recalled because he remembered additional information. He said that Saxton had told him, after the wastepaper basket incident, that he did not want her to come into his rooms, and that he should tell her to leave if she came back.

Then James Huddell, a clerk at the Hotel Federal in Alleghany, testified that he had seen Annie at his hotel on two occasions, and she and Saxton had been registered as "G.D. Smith and wife, Toledo, O." Earlier testimony had established that George Saxton had met Annie in Alleghany in order to renew his promise to marry her—if she dropped all the suits against him. When she returned to Canton, she did drop them. Other witnesses testified that Saxton and Annie had come to his farm near Sandyville, Ohio, together, on several occasions.

Jacob Adams testified that he was working at Kensington Place on the night of the murder, and around 6:00 p.m. he was on Lincoln Avenue and passed an unknown man. He said he saw George on Tuscarawas Street and spoke to him. George told him that he had seen a man halfway between Third Street and Tuscarawas Street on his way to Lincoln Avenue. On cross-examination, Adams said he had gotten out of work at 6:00 p.m., and he stayed at Lang's for about half an hour. Later, Lizzie Miller testified that she had also seen a mysterious man in the area of the murder that night, but she could not positively identify him.

J.H. Reigner, who was now justice of the peace, testified that he had been a reporter for the *News-Democrat* in November 1895. He said that he had transcribed letters from George Saxton to Annie, word for word, and they were published in the newspaper at that time. The defense moved to enter the copies into evidence. The state objected, but they were admitted. Welty read them aloud to the jury, including one that talked specifically about Annie's pending divorce and her husband's lawsuit against George:

Canton, O, April 30, 1892

Dear Anna,
I wrote you last Wednesday, and I suppose that you think I am scolding you all of the time, but I do not want to scold you because I guess you have enough trouble without scolding from me. I will send Grant down to

Hanoverton on the 9th of next month to see the witnesses and have a talk with them and take their depositions. I do not think you are going to have any trouble with your case out there, but of course I do not know what Sample's arguments are, but I do not think he cares whether you get a divorce or not if he can only get some money on the other case. I will want to take your deposition in relation to the letter and offer that Sample made. You told me that he offered me for $1,000 if you would go before his attorney and say that I was the cause of your leaving him. Was that what the letter said? If we only had that letter it would be valuable evidence.

With love and kisses,
George

Later, when M.C. Barber took the stand on behalf of his wife, George's sister Mary, who was too ill to appear in court, he stated that no receipt for George's settlement with Annie's husband had been found in his estate papers.

The defense then called Annie and Sample George's seventeen-year-old son, Newton George, to the stand. He was now living in Alliance with his father but testified about his time living with both his parents and his brother Howard in the Saxton block when he was five or six years old. They moved around a bit and returned to the Saxton block after his parents separated. "I saw Mr. Saxton nearly every day or night while we lived in Room 7, at all times of the day," he said. When asked if he received any presents from George, he said, "Yes, he gave me a bank and gave us candy." He also told the court his mother had often received candy and flowers from him. He continued to describe the arrangements when they returned to the Saxton block: "Howard and I slept in the dining room or kitchen. Saxton was about there at night. Mr. Saxton would order my brother and me to bed early in the evening. Once he told us, after we went to bed, to keep quiet and not make noise in the block. Mother and Saxton seemed friendly. She sometimes sat on his lap. They went riding together."

The final witness for the defense was Annie's ex-husband. The *Repository* reported that her attorney sat on the corner of the counsel table, obstructing her view of him on the witness stand. "She made no effort to see the witness," the story said. "Her face was partly turned from the stand and her chin rested on her hand, in which a handkerchief was held during all of the testimony. She only looked up once or twice." Sample testified that his marriage was "pleasant and happy" until Annie met George Saxton. They separated in 1889, but before that things were "always pleasant except the ordinary troubles between a man and his wife."

The remainder of the trial was taken up with rebuttal testimony to prove or disprove points that had been raised earlier by both sides of the case, such as whether or not Lizzie Miller considered herself a "spiritualist" and how that might have influenced her "strange impression" of the mysterious man she claimed to have seen after learning of the murder. Miller was too ill to appear in court, as verified by her physician, so that line of questioning was ultimately not addressed. County Surveyor J.H. Hoover testified about the locations and distances between certain parts of town where Annie had been seen the night of the murder. His testimony was designed to prove that Annie could have started from the murder scene and reached Florence Klinger's home on Marion Street in the time frame Klinger had stated. Pomerene asked for a map of the city to be admitted into evidence that could trace the routes referred to in the testimony, but the defense objected and it was not allowed.

Mrs. Eckroate's morphine use was examined yet again. Dr. A.C. Grant shared a lengthy list of health statistics, showing that her pulse and temperature were normal and her eyesight was good. He also said he did not observe any trembling or jerking, or unsteadiness when she walked. Dr. A.B. Walker testified that she did not have any symptoms that would indicate excessive use of morphine. Sample George was recalled to identify the memoranda of settlement between himself and George Saxton, showing that he was in receipt of $1,825 before the murder. It was admitted "after considerable controversy."

The state wanted to admit into evidence an affidavit signed in connection with Sample's lawsuit in 1891, which stated that Annie had said that she did not leave her husband because Saxton wanted her to leave him, but because of his "cruelty to her." They wanted to use it to show that Annie's state of mind was much different from the "frenzy and grief" the defense had tried to show earlier in the trial. It was not admitted on the grounds that it was "too remote from the homicide at issue to have a bearing theron." The strategy of Annie's attorneys was a general denial via a not guilty plea, but they did want the jury to hear testimony throughout the trial about her emotional state when the alleged threats against George's life occurred.

Next came closing arguments, and all four attorneys spoke. Grant went first, followed by both of Annie's attorneys. Pomerene was the last to speak. The judge warned the audience that applause or any other kind of outburst would not be tolerated. According to the *Repository*, attorney Grant's closing argument emphasized that at no time had a "homicide been denied and that the broken promises and the grief and frenzy this breach of promise had provoked were only admitted in mitigation of the degree of the crime. He insisted that the introduction of such testimony by the defense in this case constituted a confession and could only be considered as mitigation of the offense thus confessed." Furthermore, Grant argued, Annie's attorneys did not dispute that she made threats against George's life. He spent a lot of time reviewing these threats, which he noted were not threats to sue or threats to argue, but threats to kill. Next, he reviewed the testimony of Annie's former attorney, William O. Werntz, who said that Annie had discussed what effect killing George would have on her ex-husband's lawsuit. This, he said, was proof that the murder was premeditated. Grant dismissed Lizzie Miller's sighting of a mysterious figure in the vicinity of the murder scene, saying, "This is a large city, gentlemen. There are many streets and many people walk along the streets."

In closing remarks on Annie's behalf, Sterling revisited the idea of these threats. He said that the jury must first establish that she committed a murder before considering any threats. He said that the state failed to provide any proof that after leaving the streetcar at Hazlet Avenue, Annie headed in the direction of Lincoln Avenue. He repeated the argument that the car was running late that night, and she could not have gotten to the scene of the crime in time to commit the murder. He argued that placing her at the scene at the exact time was not proven by evidence "beyond all reasonable doubt." Then he indicted George Saxton's character, saying, "It is my deliberate judgement that the death of George D. Saxton was to Canton a public benefaction. That the air is purer by his passing away and our wives and sisters and daughters are safer because of his spirit taking its flight." Next, he lamented the fact that Mrs. Althouse could not be found to testify, noting that she could have shed a great deal of light on the case. He revisited the supposed eyewitness testimony, saying that the darkness of the night made it impossible for anyone to positively identify Annie as the person who fired the shots. Again he refuted the doctors who said Mrs. Eckroate did not exhibit signs of a morphine addict: "Doctors know just how much of the stuff to give to produce the desired result; they knew how to patch her up so she could walk a chalk line and pass the examination....And then [she said] she looked through the opening and saw and recognized with her aged and defective eyes what could not be recognized by the younger eyes of her daughter; the unimpaired eyes of young Hogan who couldn't tell whether the form was that of a man or a woman." The beginning of Welty's part of the defense's closing argument was characterized by the *Repository* as "justification of what Mrs. George might have done." The rest of his remarks centered on her plea of "not guilty," claiming the evidence against her was all circumstantial and that the links in the chain were "weak or missing." He reminded the jury that Annie was innocent until proven guilty, and she was entitled to the "benefit of every doubt, and so long as any of you have any doubt about any of the links in the chain she must continue to be regarded innocent." He portrayed Annie as someone who wanted to marry George, not kill him. Welty dismissed her threats as those made by an emotional woman who was desperately in love. "She loved Saxton," he said. "He had won her affection and her love completely, and she was devoted to him. She had no hatred for him; no reason to kill him, but a desire to live only for him and with him. Threats made under such circumstances were never made with the intention of executing them." Welty also urged the jury not to trust the testimony of Mrs. Eckroate, saying, "If Mrs. Eckroate saw Mrs. George wouldn't she have said so that night, when everybody was looking for her?" He also took one final opportunity to remind the jury of her alleged morphine addiction, adding, "As the experts say, when morphine is there the brain is diseased and the mind irresponsible."

Pomerene was the last to speak. He took issue with Sterling's commentary regarding George Saxton's death. "I sat there appalled when I heard my Brother Sterling say that that man was rightfully killed," he said. "An attorney at the bar justifying a cruel murder! I do not believe any juror will so decide." He went on to say that the matter at hand was whether or not they had proven beyond a reasonable doubt that she was guilty, which had nothing to do with "how dark they have painted the character of Saxton." He refuted the idea that the timeline was not sufficient for Annie to get off the streetcar at Hazlett and arrive at Mrs. Althouse's address within the established timeframe of the murder. He also revisited the testimony of Lizzie Miller. "We did not get a chance to finish her cross-examination," he said. "But let us see. She thought she saw a woman, then a man and then it faded away. She said she had a strange impression. I don't know whether she had just come out of a trance or not, but I suspect this ghost story will not be believed by you. The things the defense have attempted to prove show the weakness of their case as well as do things they have left unproven."

The trial ended at 11:50 a.m. on Thursday, April 27, and was handed over to the jury. They received a lengthy list of instructions from Judge Taylor, including the difference between first-degree murder, second-degree murder and manslaughter. The jurors were reminded that the fact that

EXTRA.
NOT GUILTY.
The Jury's Verdict In the George Case.
How It Was Received At the Court House.

THE STATE OF OHIO, ? In the Court of Common
   Stark County, ss. } Pleas of Said County,
                          January T., A. D. 1899.

THE STATE OF OHIO, Plaintiff, ?
          Against   } Criminal Action.
ANNA E. GEORGE, Defendant. }

We, the Jury impanneled and sworn to well and truly try, and true deliverance make between the State of Ohio and the prisoner at the bar, Anna E. George, do find the defendant not guilty.

Julius A. Zang, Foreman.

Headline, "Extra. Not Guilty." When the jury announced a verdict of not guilty, the audience in the courtroom broke into loud cheers. This headline appeared in the April 28, 1899 edition of the *Repository. Courtesy of the* Repository.

Annie did not testify on her own behalf was not to be considered evidence against her. The judge also said that if they had any reasonable doubt about her guilt after reviewing and weighing all of the evidence presented to them at the trial, they must find her not guilty. The jury was sequestered on the third floor of the courthouse, where they were "not again allowed to separate or to leave...until a verdict has been found or the court is convinced that no verdict can be found." Spectators remained in the courtroom until after midnight. As they deliberated, the men could be seen through the window of the room in which they were ensconced. The *Repository* reported that "shirt sleeves were de rigeur at an early stage of the deliberations." As the night progressed, the men were seen pacing the room, and many removed vests, collars and ties.

At 10:42 a.m. on Friday, April 28, the jury returned to the courtroom, and the foreman announced that they found Annie George not guilty. In spite of Judge Taylor's directive that there should be no demonstration after the verdict was announced, there were loud cheers in the courtroom. "Half a score of women rushed to Mrs. George and congratulated her," the *Repository* said. "She hurried to the jury box, took each man by the hand and gave him a word and a nod of thanks." The next day, the *Repository* printed reactions from newspapers across northeastern Ohio and western Pennsylvania. The *Alliance Review* wrote, "The verdict of not guilty will be variously received, for the belief has been almost universal that she committed the deed. Equally general is the feeling that the man who was slain had given her extreme provocation."

Speaking on behalf of George Saxton's family, M.C. Barber said they were not at all pleased with the verdict, according to the *Stark County Democrat*.

"We haven't had a fair show," he said. "The court has been against us, and a manufactured public opinion has been against us from the outset. Now, understand we are not quarreling with the verdict. If that woman goes her way and bothers us no more, and does not come back to Canton and gloat over her escape from a just punishment, we will be content."

In the days after the trial, Annie received telegrams and letters of congratulations from near and far. She could not walk down the street without being greeted by well-wishers. She received an offer to appear in a drama on the stage, which she declined, but she ultimately accepted an offer to share her story on the lecture circuit. Reportedly, she expected standing-room-only crowds, but her lectures were not well attended, so she discontinued them. She went back to her vocation as a seamstress and for a time had a dress shop on Market Avenue in Canton. Then Annie faded into history, and little is known about her life after the trial.

8

JAMES CORNELIUS

On Monday, September 17, 1906, the front-page headline of the *Repository* screamed, "KILLED WIFE WITH WEIGHT, Cantonian Admits Guilt." The first paragraph read, "James Cornelius, sewer contractor, brutally murdered his wife early Monday·morning, at the family home on South Market Street, by beating her on the head with a heavy 10-inch iron window weight. She died at Aultman Hospital a few hours after the tragedy. Cornelius is in jail, a self-confessed murderer." After striking his wife, Estella, James left their home and walked up Market Avenue, stopping to buy a cigar. When he saw police coming for him, he turned on a side street but surrendered peaceably when confronted. As his wife lay dying, he "coolly expressed the hope that his victim might die."

Police had been called to 1943 South Market Avenue at 6:55 a.m. via telephone. When they arrived on the scene, they found Estella Cornelius lying in a pool of blood. She had been struck with a window weight that weighed several pounds. Her skull had been crushed. She never regained consciousness and was pronounced dead at the hospital around 10:30 a.m.

Her estranged husband was no stranger to law enforcement. Just one week before the murder, James had been arrested for "being intoxicated and creating a disturbance." The *Repository* reported that according to their neighbors, the couple had gotten into a loud argument the previous Saturday night. James had broken one of the doors in the house, but "the trouble seemed to have quieted down, and no arrest was made." The neighbors said they often heard them fighting and James frequently used "harsh" language. "It is evident," the article said, "according to the statements of a neighbor, that one of those quarrels was in progress when the murder was committed."

One neighbor, Mrs. Frank McCausland, told the *Repository* that Estella recently expressed concern that James would kidnap their two young sons, Dean, eleven, and James, two. She also said he had threatened to go to Wooster to disinter the body of another son who had died three years earlier and not tell her where he moved the body. She was so worried about his threat, she actually went to Wooster to speak to the cemetery superintendent to see if he would be allowed to do it. She had said that when they were fighting, he often threatened to kill her, and she would say that she would "have the pleasure of being buried beside her son's body in Wooster." He allegedly told her that he would "see that her desire was not gratified; that he would have the body moved to some place unknown."

Estella had an eighteen-year-old daughter, Florence, from a previous relationship, who had seen James attack her mother. Florence told police that her mother and stepfather were not fighting before he struck her. "I was standing upon the back porch, only a few feet from those on the inside," she said, "and I saw father strike mother over the shoulder with the big piece of iron, but I did not see him strike the blow that crushed her head. I ran screaming for help, and for this reason did not see mamma killed by her brutal husband. He was always of a brutal disposition and when in liquor was unbearable." James initially claimed that Estella had accused him of having an intimate relationship with her daughter, but Florence said he was lying about that. "There is no truth in the story whatever," she said. "He has awfully treated my mother, and hanging and the electric chair are too easy for him." The case was given directly to the grand jury, bypassing a preliminary hearing in front of the mayor. The jury indicted James with murder in the first degree, and his trial was scheduled for November 19.

The *Stark County Democrat* declared it "one of the most brutal murders ever committed in Canton." The newspaper printed some of the backstory in the September 21 edition. James and Estella had moved from Wooster to Canton eighteen months earlier. He made good money as a contractor but reportedly did not use much of his income to support his family. On August 30, Estella had filed for divorce on the grounds of "extreme cruelty." Two weeks before the murder, "the couple came to an understanding by which it was agreed that Cornelius was to come back on trial and should he conduct himself differently the charges would be dropped. How well he kept his promise the dead body of his wife bears mute testimony."

On the Saturday before the murder, James made good on his threat to kidnap Dean and James when he snatched them from the front yard. Estella immediately called the police, but the trio disappeared. The next day, Estella received a call from her sister-in-law in Shreve, Ohio, who said the children were with her. She told Estella "if she did not call for them at once they would be placed in a children's home as she did not want to support them. To this Mrs. Cornelius is said to have replied she could do so as they would be better off than at home."

On Sunday night, neighbor J.M. Turner saw James at the house around 7:30 p.m. Estella saw him coming, locked the door and refused to let him in. They fought through the door for about ten minutes, and then he went around the house and kicked the back door down. Estella walked out the front door and down the street. Turner said he asked James if his wife was afraid of him. He said he replied, "Yes, but she needn't be. She is the only one I ever loved and I wouldn't harm a hair on her head." Turner said he repeated it several times, which he found odd. In retrospect, Turner thought James had come to the house with the intent to murder Estella on Sunday night, but after drawing so much attention to himself, he changed his mind. The *Stark County Democrat* also reported that James was a known coward, which was "clearly demonstrated by the time he chose to commit the crime when all the men in the neighborhood had gone to work."

The trial began on Monday, November 19, as scheduled. As with many of the cases we have seen, selecting a jury was an arduous task. By Wednesday, the following men were seated as jurors: E.J. Meyers, Phillip Heidrich, A.L. McDonald, L.A. Reddy, George Sponseller, W.L. Nash, Ed Gleitsman, Frank Killing, George Leiper, John Berkholder, C.A. Ream and J.H. Palmer. Charles C. Upham served as prosecutor, the defense attorneys were John C. Welty and J.W. Albaugh and Judge Harter presided.

In his opening statement, Welty said James had committed the murder while intoxicated and "smarting beneath a charge made by his wife concerning his actions toward her daughter Florence." He painted a picture of James as a loving father and husband who had gone awry because of his drinking. "The proof will show that the husband drank whiskey by the quart and gallon prior to the time of the deed," he said. "When trouble and disappointment came he drank more and more." His attorney claimed that James was trying to reconcile with his wife, not kill her.

The first witness called by the state was Florence. She spent two and a half hours on the stand. She testified that one week before the murder, she and her mother had gone upstairs to bed. James called Estella back downstairs, and they both went down. James asked her mother where the revolver was, and she replied that it was in the creek. He told Florence to go up to bed, but her mother told her to stay. "Sticking his finger under my nose he ordered me to bed and said that he would slap me if I did not go," she said. "I refused and he struck me in the face twice. I ran out of the house and called the police." For the rest of the week, Florence, her fifteen-year-old brother, Ross, and her mother slept in one room together.

On the Saturday before the murder, Florence had scrubbed the kitchen, the room where her mother would soon be killed, and she said there was no window weight in the room. On Monday morning, her mother and Ross were in the kitchen eating breakfast. James was also in the room drinking coffee. Ross left for work. James told Estella he wanted her to go to Shreve, where the younger children were, and she said she would consult her lawyer first. James went outside and then came back in. He said something about "putting himself where he'd harm nobody," and Estella said she didn't care what he did as long as she was left alone. According to Florence, he picked up the window weight and said to her mother, "Do you see this?" Estella did not answer. Then Florence saw him hit her with it three times before she ran screaming from the house to find help. She went to Kennedy's grocery store and called the police. After seeing James leave the house, she went back home and found her mother lying on the kitchen floor in a pool of her own blood.

Upon cross-examination, Florence admitted there were between twenty-five and fifty empty whiskey bottles on the back porch. "Generally he was a staggering drunk," she said. Welty asked her if Estella had accused James of incest that morning, which she vehemently denied. On redirect, Florence said that James had appeared sober just before the murder. Mrs. J.T. Bucher, who had seen James a few minutes after the murder, corroborated Florence's testimony, saying he was "acting as if he had full possession of his senses."

The defense intended to show that years of drunkenness had "diseased" James's mind and that his mental condition made it impossible for him to plan a murder. The defense hoped to prove that he was not capable of committing murder in the first or second degree. He did not deny killing her, so the goal was a conviction of manslaughter, which carried a lesser sentence.

The first witnesses for the defense were two brothers who owned a saloon. They said James had come for a drink at 6:00 a.m. on the day of the murder, and they had given him a glass of whiskey and "probably a beer." Next, a string of medical experts was called to testify about "alcoholic insanity."

According to the *Stark County Democrat*, Upham asked Dr. Brant, "Doctor, isn't it a fact that some men can drink more than others?" Dr. Brant said yes. "Now, doctor," Upham continued, "anybody who ever read history, knows that Daniel Webster was a hard drinker for 40 years; now, doctor, do you think he was insane?" Welty objected, and Judge Harter overruled. The doctor was permitted to reply, "No, sir, I would not call him insane." Upham continued this line of questioning, and Dr. Brand admitted that some men could drink to excess yet still were able enough to work, pay their bills and conduct regular business.

Dr. Eyman, superintendent of the Massillon State Hospital, a facility for mental patients, had been asked to evaluate James to determine whether or not he was sane. Approximately eight hundred patients under Dr. Eyman's care were placed in the hospital for alcoholic insanity. Upham asked him if, in his opinion, James was sane. Welty immediately objected on the grounds that James had been forced into the examination without his own attorney present and that he could not be compelled to testify against himself in this way. After considerable debate, Judge Harter allowed the testimony to continue, and Dr. Eyman said that he found James to be sane. Two other experts—Dr. Marchand and Dr. E.J. March—also examined James and found him to be sane. Attorney W.J. Piero, whom Estella had hired to begin divorce proceedings, testified that he had met with the accused several times regarding the case in the three weeks prior to the murder and he "had not conducted himself otherwise than as a sane man."

Before closing arguments began on Friday, November 30, Judge Harter instructed the jury about the difference between a civil and a criminal case and explained in detail the difference between murder in the first degree, murder in the second degree and manslaughter. First degree required intent, second degree meant that he simply killed her and manslaughter could be the result of "an outburst of sudden passion or a quarrel." He told the jury that they had the right to consider the role alcoholism might have played in the defendant's mental capacity to plan his wife's murder.

In his closing argument, assistant prosecutor McCulloch said that no testimony had been presented regarding Estella's character as a wife or mother. "She did her duty always," he said in the *Repository*. "On the other hand we find the defendant was a heavy drinker and that three weeks previous to the crime the wife filed petition for divorce, finding it impossible to live with him any longer. She had full made up her mind to separate from him forever." James had begged her to take him back, which, among other things, McCullough said was evidence that he was, indeed, sane.

Albaugh spoke first for the defense:

We come into this court admitting the defendant was the cause of the killing. We say that when he struck the fatal blows he was in such condition of mind to make him an absolute of pity. It was no ridiculous farce, this defense of ours. Cornelius drank enough whiskey to undermine his vitals. This is not a trumped up charge. Testimony has been presented to show he drank enough liquor to kill almost any man. This case can be almost taken as a temperance lecture. I do not have any respect for a man who imbibes to over indulgence in liquor....Cornelius had been drunk for days, weeks, months and years before he committed this crime. Think of downing a quart of whiskey a day....The man's mind was diseased and when in that state he was a brute.

Then it was Welty's turn. He argued that the only charge that could be proven against his client was manslaughter, due to his alcoholism. "Gentleman," he said, "I do not desire the guilty to go unpunished....If the defendant is guilty it is for you to say. In cases such as this the presumption is always with the defendant in the degree of proof which must be higher than in any other charge. This is a case which needs to be handled with intelligence. The jury should analyze and think. If it is true the defendant was in the habit of using alcohol all the time he is a subject for pity, for if there is anything we should be thankful for it is reason. Take that element away from us and we would want to die." Welty added that he did not think Florence was a reliable witness, pointing out that she admitted she was not on speaking terms with her stepfather.

After just five hours of deliberation, the jury found James Cornelius guilty of first-degree murder on December 4. On December 22, Judge Harter sentenced him to death by electric chair, making him the first Stark County resident to be put to death in that manner. James told the *Repository* that he was not interested in having his sentence commuted to life in prison. "I want to die," he said. "My wife's dead and I haven't anything to live for." He was transported immediately to the state penitentiary, where he would await his execution. Deputy Sherriff Adam Oberlin accompanied him to the state prison and told the *Repository* that James "talked incessantly about his trial." He said he "would not be happy until he was with his wife."

While awaiting his execution, James wrote a letter to Florence, and it was published in the *Repository* on June 2, 1907. In part, he said, "There is about ten days that I don't remember but very little that happened and I thank God that I can't. I would love to see you and Ross and have a talk with you before I leave this world. My time is not long on this world, but I will be glad when it is over for I know that I will be with the one we all loved so well that is in heaven."

The execution was delayed several times, but ultimately Governor Andrew L. Harris, who was opposed to the death penalty, chose not to intervene in his case. The *Cleveland Plain Dealer* reported that the governor had spent "hours day and night in going over every portion of the testimony and law in the case. Until the last minute he held his final decision open, that additional affidavits in support of a life sentence might be presented." The governor noted that during the trial, five of the six doctors called as experts determined that James knew right from wrong. In the *Repository* on the day before the execution, Governor Harris said, "Whatever my personal opinion on capital punishment may be, and however deeply I may feel the responsibility resting upon me, I must enforce the law as I find it. The execution of the sentence will not be disturbed."

James had nothing to say before climbing into the electric chair just after midnight on June 28, 1907. According to the *Plain Dealer*, "If there was any emotion playing with Cornelius's heart he kept it well concealed. With light step he approached the grim chair and jauntily he stepped in. His face was immobile as he sat down. It did not pale; not a muscle quivered." At 12:04 a.m., the electric current was turned on, and five and a half minutes later, James was dead. He had requested to be buried next to his wife and their son, but his brothers thought Estella's family would object. Instead, he was buried alone in Wooster.

ABOUT THE AUTHOR

Kim Kenney earned her Master of Arts degree in History Museum Studies at the Cooperstown Graduate Program in New York. She became curator of the McKinley Presidential Library & Museum in 2001 and was promoted to executive director in 2019. She has authored eight books, and her work has appeared in *The Public Historian, White House History, the Repository*, the *Boston Globe, Aviation History* and *Mused*. Kim has appeared on *The Daily Show, First Ladies: Influence & Images* and *Mysteries at the Museum*. Her program "The 1918 Influenza Pandemic" was featured on C-SPAN's series *American History TV*.